HISTORY OF THE WORLD IN COMICS

TABLE OF CONTENTS

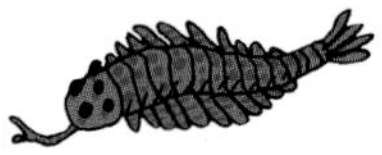

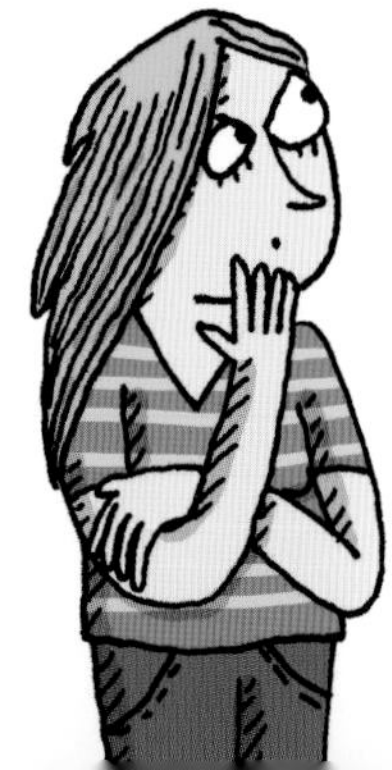

HISTORY OF THE WORLD IN COMICS

by Jean-Baptiste de Panafieu • illustrated by Adrienne Barman

HOLIDAY HOUSE · NEW YORK

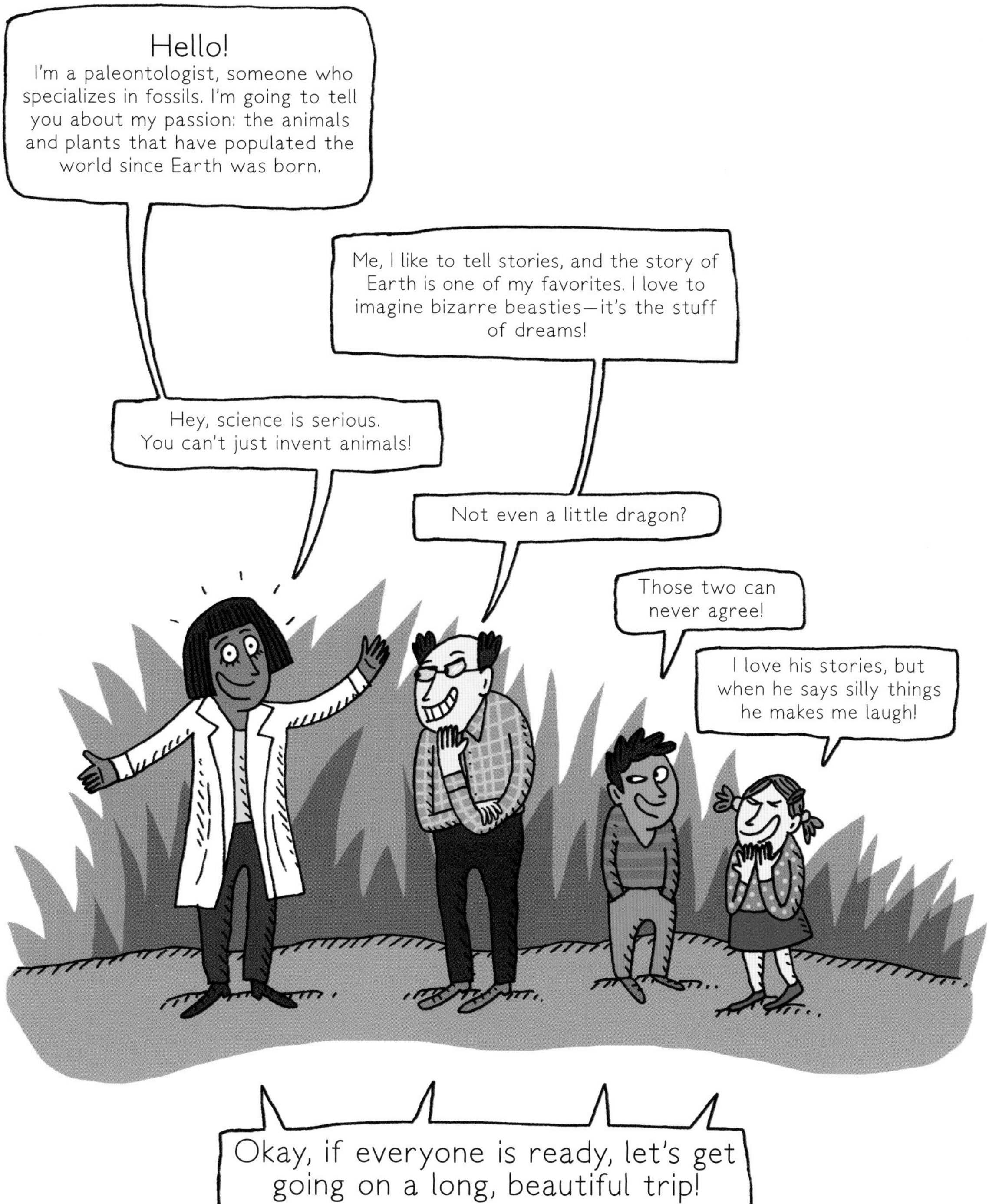
Hello! I'm a paleontologist, someone who specializes in fossils. I'm going to tell you about my passion: the animals and plants that have populated the world since Earth was born.
Me, I like to tell stories, and the story of Earth is one of my favorites. I love to imagine bizarre beasties—it's the stuff of dreams!
Hey, science is serious. You can't just invent animals!
Not even a little dragon?
Those two can never agree!
I love his stories, but when he says silly things he makes me laugh!
Okay, if everyone is ready, let's get going on a long, beautiful trip!

A very long time ago, somewhere in infinite space . . .

Try to be a little more precise. It happened 4.6 billion years ago, at the edge of our galaxy.

Yes, this is no fairy tale!

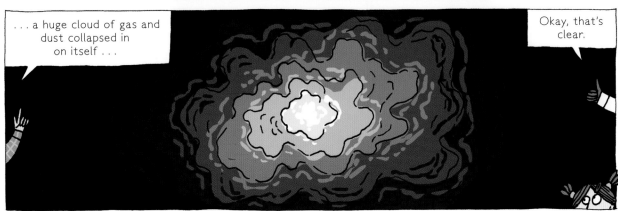

. . . a huge cloud of gas and dust collapsed in on itself . . .

Okay, that's clear.

. . . and gave birth to our solar system.

In the middle was the sun, and rotating around it was a disk made up of countless bits of debris, which little by little stuck to each other and formed several large masses . . .

I get it, those were what would become the planets. . . .

And that's how our wonderful planet, Earth, was born . . .

. . . but it wasn't habitable, because it was still a burning ball of lava at more than 2,200 degrees Fahrenheit!

. . . and don't forget the other planets—Mars, Venus . . .

. . . and Mercury and Jupiter and Saturn and . . .

Yes, yes, we get it!

THE PRECAMBRIAN
4.6 billion to 540 million years ago

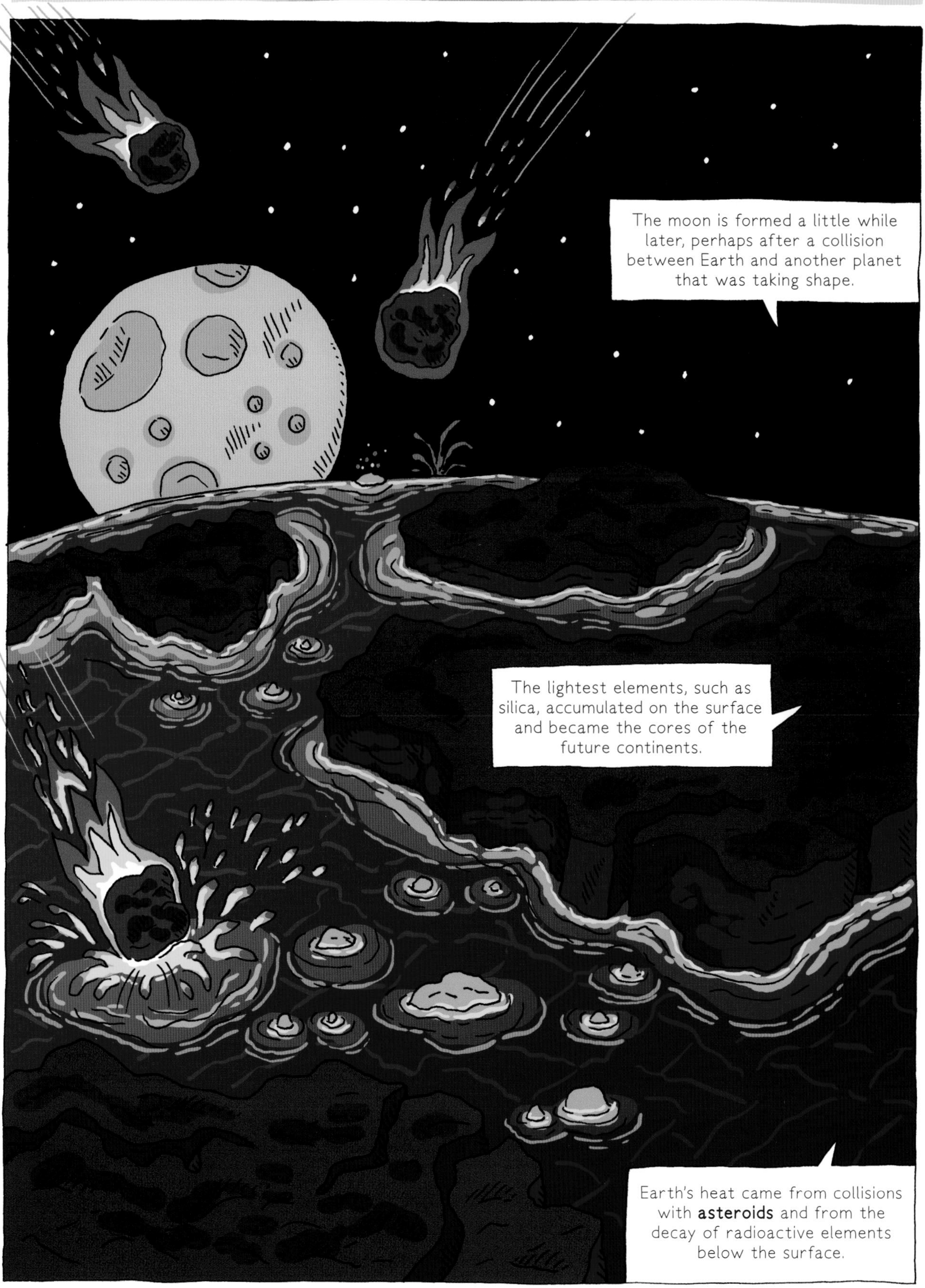
The moon is formed a little while later, perhaps after a collision between Earth and another planet that was taking shape.
The lightest elements, such as silica, accumulated on the surface and became the cores of the future continents.
Earth's heat came from collisions with **asteroids** and from the decay of radioactive elements below the surface.

The period from 4.6 billion to 4 billion years ago is called the **Hadean**, from the Greek word for the underworld, Hades.

It's really infernal!

Yes, but it doesn't last! A solid crust forms on the surface. It's often broken by currents stirring the **magma** and by falling **meteorites**.

Earth cools. The magma becomes more viscous and the crust thickens. The atmosphere contains nitrogen, carbon dioxide, methane, and water vapor. When its temperature drops to 212 degrees Fahrenheit, rain begins to fall.

Those first drops of boiling rain are the beginning of the oceans!

About 4.3 billion years ago, water covered a large portion of Earth. It came from the rocky magma and from meteorites.

That sounds more hospitable!

Living creatures may have appeared at this time. But . . .

. . . between 4 billion and 3.8 billion years ago, Earth experienced a huge bombardment of meteorites. The crust probably melted again, and the oceans evaporated completely before conditions stabilized.

I don't see how animals or even **microbes** could have survived!

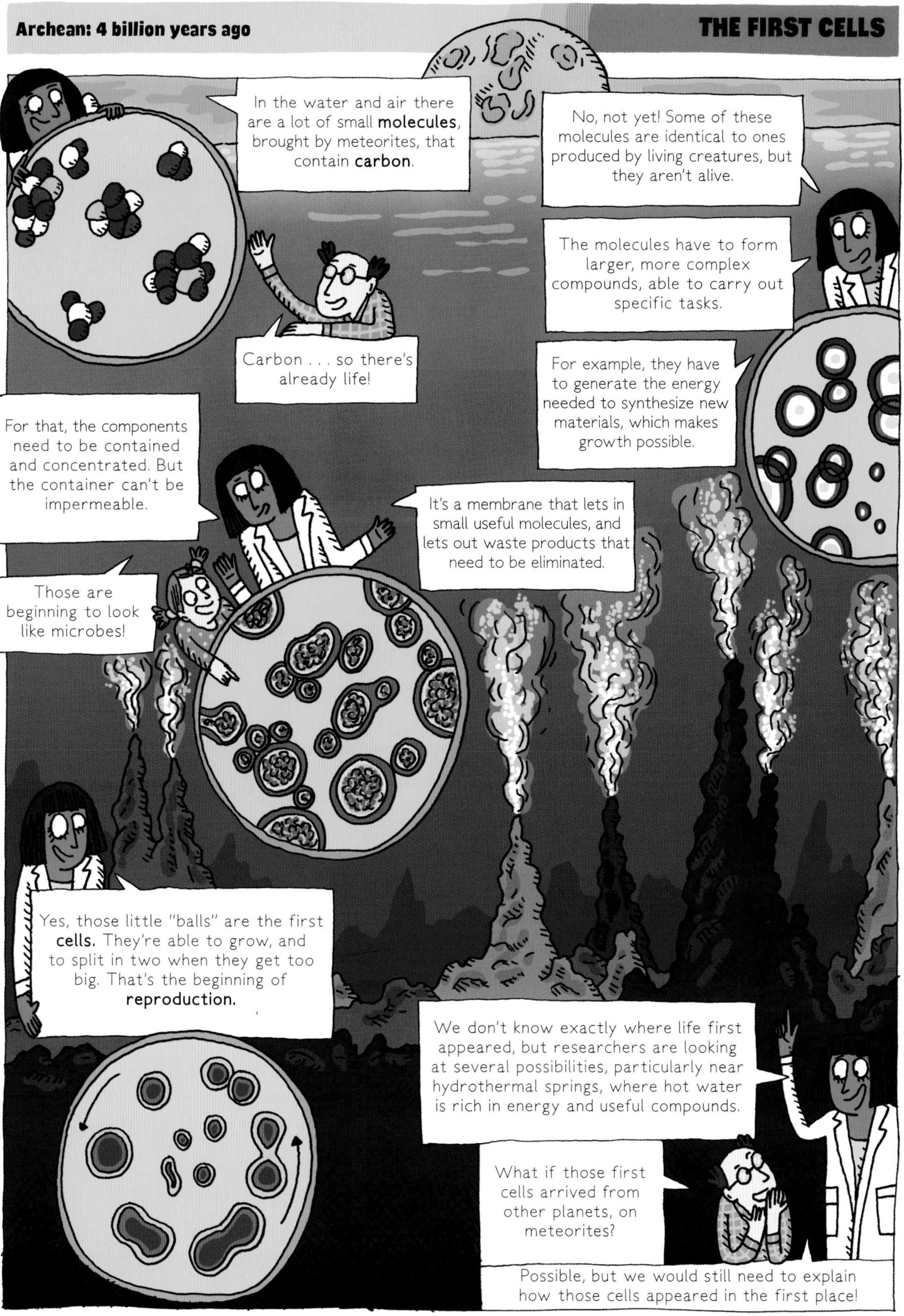
In the water and air there are a lot of small **molecules**, brought by meteorites, that contain **carbon**.
Carbon . . . so there's already life!
No, not yet! Some of these molecules are identical to ones produced by living creatures, but they aren't alive.
The molecules have to form larger, more complex compounds, able to carry out specific tasks.
For example, they have to generate the energy needed to synthesize new materials, which makes growth possible.
For that, the components need to be contained and concentrated. But the container can't be impermeable.
It's a membrane that lets in small useful molecules, and lets out waste products that need to be eliminated.
Those are beginning to look like microbes!
Yes, those little "balls" are the first **cells.** They're able to grow, and to split in two when they get too big. That's the beginning of **reproduction.**
We don't know exactly where life first appeared, but researchers are looking at several possibilities, particularly near hydrothermal springs, where hot water is rich in energy and useful compounds.
What if those first cells arrived from other planets, on meteorites?
Possible, but we would still need to explain how those cells appeared in the first place!

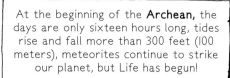

At the beginning of the **Archean,** the days are only sixteen hours long, tides rise and fall more than 300 feet (100 meters), meteorites continue to strike our planet, but Life has begun!

The first cells change rapidly as they divide.

Changes that are useful for survival are kept, while those that are harmful are quickly eliminated. It's the beginning of **evolution.**

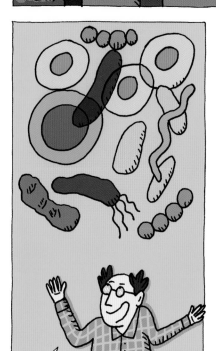

One of these primitive microbes will have an extraordinary destiny, since it will give rise to all the creatures living today!

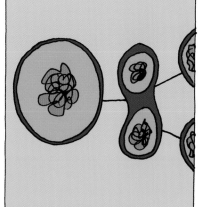

Yes, it's called **LUCA**—the last universal common ancestor.

And after that, everything moves very quickly . . .

. . . well, in evolutionary time, which is counted in hundreds of millions of years!

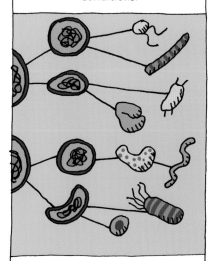

At least two lines appear: the **bacteria** and the **archaea.** They're very similar, but the archaea can live in extreme conditions.

These two lines still live among us, in the soil, in the water . . .

. . . and in our intestines!

Three and a half billion years ago, bacteria produced limestone that was laid down in thin layers on the rocks. This created **stromatolites,** stones shaped like columns or mushrooms. Some of them still exist in Australia.

There is almost no oxygen in the atmosphere. **Microorganisms** get the energy they need by other means.

Some of them use solar energy. They expel a product that, for them, is toxic waste: **oxygen**!

The accumulation of this gas in the atmosphere is accompanied by cooling that affects almost the entire planet. It becomes "snowball Earth."

Then the **glaciation** ends and the atmosphere warms up again.

Fortunately!

Another thing that's new is that certain bacteria learn to use oxygen, which gives them more energy and lets them form larger organisms.

We don't know whether these are colonies of bacteria or true animals.

Gabonionta

Animals?

DNA

Yes, something else very important happens! Some of the microorganisms become specialized and eat others. Sometimes the one that is swallowed is not digested, and continues to live inside the one that ate it.

These associations form a third line, the **eukaryotes,** which will give rise to all of today's animals and plants.

Repeated glaciations transform Earth into a "snowball" again and again! Each time, most of the tiny organisms that live in the oceans die en masse. But some of them survive!

And continue to evolve!

Thanks to the bacteria and microalgae, the atmosphere continues to become richer in oxygen. Cells group together and form colonies about an inch long!

Huge!

Some of the oxygen forms an ozone layer that protects Earth's surface from ultraviolet rays. Algae and fungi begin to colonize the continents.

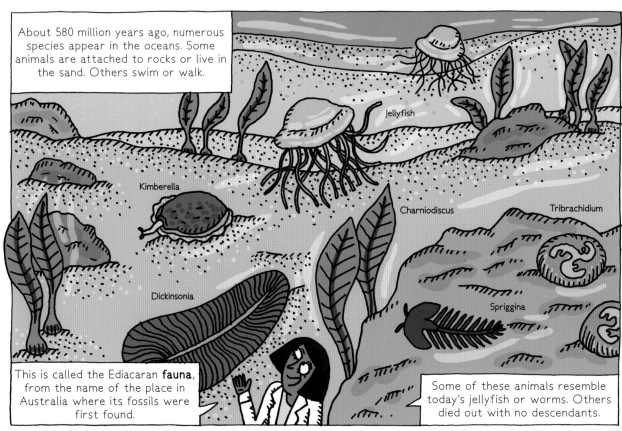

About 580 million years ago, numerous species appear in the oceans. Some animals are attached to rocks or live in the sand. Others swim or walk.

Jellyfish

Kimberella

Charniodiscus

Tribrachidium

Dickinsonia

Spriggina

This is called the Ediacaran **fauna**, from the name of the place in Australia where its fossils were first found.

Some of these animals resemble today's jellyfish or worms. Others died out with no descendants.

THE PALEOZOIC
540 million to 252 million years ago

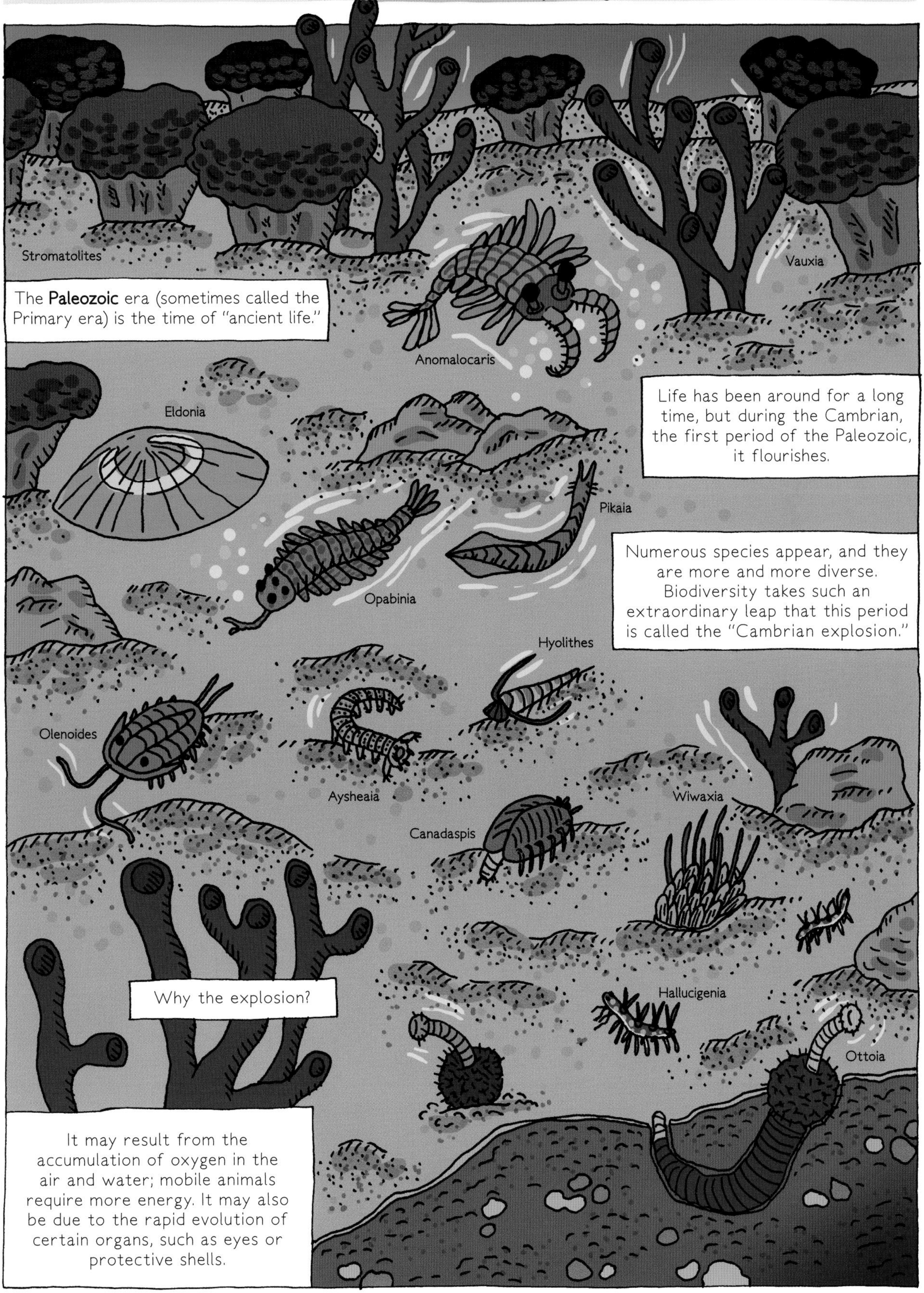
Stromatolites
Vauxia
The **Paleozoic** era (sometimes called the Primary era) is the time of "ancient life."
Anomalocaris
Eldonia
Life has been around for a long time, but during the Cambrian, the first period of the Paleozoic, it flourishes.
Pikaia
Opabinia
Numerous species appear, and they are more and more diverse. Biodiversity takes such an extraordinary leap that this period is called the "Cambrian explosion."
Hyolithes
Olenoides
Aysheaia
Wiwaxia
Canadaspis
Why the explosion?
Hallucigenia
Ottoia
It may result from the accumulation of oxygen in the air and water; mobile animals require more energy. It may also be due to the rapid evolution of certain organs, such as eyes or protective shells.

At the beginning of the **Cambrian**, the first predators appear. For the **herbivores** and the animals that eat **plankton** (small animals that drift in the ocean), life will never be the same!

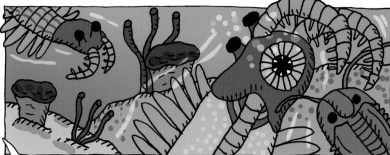

Anomalocaris grows up to 3.3 feet (1 meter) long. It's the largest predator of the time! It has compound eyes to spot its prey, which it seizes with two articulated arms bristling with spikes.

Its circular mouth is surrounded by spiny plates.

But prey species also evolve. They become more mobile and better protected.

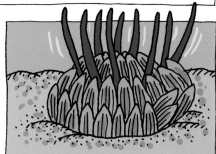

Wiwaxia nibbles on the carpet of bacteria covering the sea floor. Its body is covered with hard plates and spines.

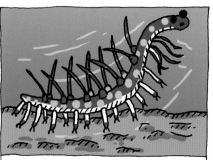

Hallucigenia moves about on pairs of legs with claws. On its back are two rows of spines.

Opabinia has five eyes on stalks, and a trunk with a pair of jaws.

It look like an extraterrestrial!

Many of these animals have no known modern equivalents. They became extinct and had no descendants.

But others seem to be the forerunners of modern species. **Haikouichthys,** for example, looks like a small fish.

It could be the ancestor of all the vertebrates.

During the Paleozoic Era, the oceans are densely populated with **trilobites** and **eurypterids**. They're predators and scavengers, like today's **crabs** and **shrimps**.

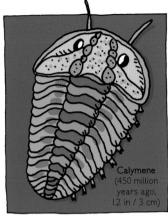

Calymene (450 million years ago, 1.2 in / 3 cm)

They're all **arthropods**. Like insects and crustaceans, the trilobites are covered by articulated shells. Some can roll themselves up for protection.

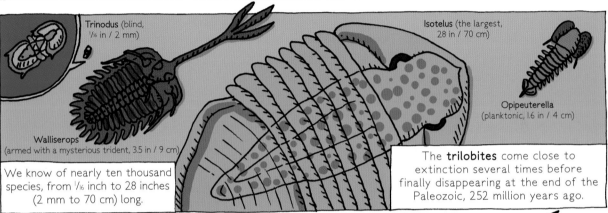

Trinodus (blind, 1/16 in / 2 mm)

Walliserops (armed with a mysterious trident, 3.5 in / 9 cm)

Isotelus (the largest, 28 in / 70 cm)

Opipeuterella (planktonic, 1.6 in / 4 cm)

We know of nearly ten thousand species, from 1/16 inch to 28 inches (2 mm to 70 cm) long.

The **trilobites** come close to extinction several times before finally disappearing at the end of the Paleozoic, 252 million years ago.

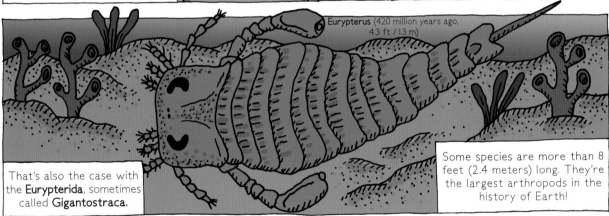

Eurypterus (420 million years ago, 4.3 ft / 1.3 m)

That's also the case with the **Eurypterida**, sometimes called **Gigantostraca**.

Some species are more than 8 feet (2.4 meters) long. They're the largest arthropods in the history of Earth!

They're sometimes called sea scorpions, but many of them lived in fresh water, and we don't know whether their pointed tails, or telsons, were venomous. They were cousins of the scorpions, not their ancestors.

Pterygotus (5.3 ft / 1.6 m)

Another of their cousins, the **horseshoe crab,** is still living!

The oceans of the Paleozoic are brimming with life, but the continents are still deserted.

Not completely! We need to look a little closer, because the inhabitants are tiny.

The most ancient terrestrial plants are small, branched stalks without leaves.

Thanks to their green **chlorophyll**, they're able to carry out **photosynthesis,** to nourish themselves with the help of solar energy.

They bear little sacs filled with spores; that's how they reproduce.

This carpet of plants attracts aquatic animals. The shells that protected them from predators now keep them from drying out and support them when they're no longer buoyed by the water.

At the beginning they're very small **arachnids, mites** or **springtails** that eat plant debris. Then they attract predators— **scorpions** and **spiders**.

Some of their descendants will be much larger.

Soon it will be the time of **giant insects** and **tree ferns!**

The tiny vertebrates of the Cambrian, like **Haikouichthys,** have evolved. About 470 million years ago, larger species appear.

They look a little like fish, but their bodies are protected by heavy armor.

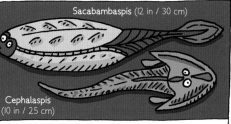

Sacabambaspis (12 in / 30 cm)

Cephalaspis (10 in / 25 cm)

Only their tails are mobile. What's more, they don't have jaws!

They can't eat?

Yes, of course they can! They have mouths, and they suck in small animals that live on the bottom.

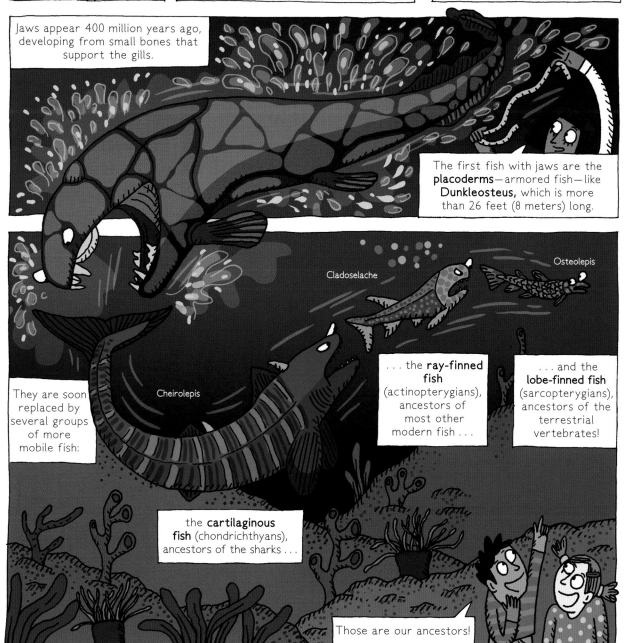

Jaws appear 400 million years ago, developing from small bones that support the gills.

The first fish with jaws are the **placoderms**—armored fish—like **Dunkleosteus,** which is more than 26 feet (8 meters) long.

Cladoselache

Osteolepis

Cheirolepis

They are soon replaced by several groups of more mobile fish:

... the **ray-finned fish** (actinopterygians), ancestors of most other modern fish . . .

... and the **lobe-finned fish** (sarcopterygians), ancestors of the terrestrial vertebrates!

the **cartilaginous fish** (chondrichthyans), ancestors of the sharks . . .

Those are our ancestors!

A fierce predatory fish, **Eusthenopteron**, lived 380 million years ago in the marshes of the vast coastal plains.

It hunts and devours smaller fish, the **acanthodians**.

Eusthenopteron is not like other fish. It isn't even really a fish!

It has rudimentary lungs, which allow it to breathe air on the surface when the water is too muddy.

Its fins are supported by bones and muscles, like real limbs.

It uses them to paddle in shallow water by pushing against the bottom.

Its fins are like those of the **coelacanth**, which lives in the Indian Ocean!

A few million years later, a related species, **Tiktaalik**, has articulated fins with elbows. It can lift itself onto the bank!

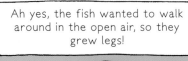

Ah yes, the fish wanted to walk around in the open air, so they grew legs!

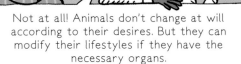

Not at all! Animals don't change at will according to their desires. But they can modify their lifestyles if they have the necessary organs.

During the Devonian, numerous species succeed one another. One is **Acanthostega**, which has true limbs, with four feet!

Thanks to its feet and its lungs, it can find new sources of food—on terra firma!

Yum, delicious millipedes!

Acanthostega's feet have eight digits. But other species have five.

Like me!

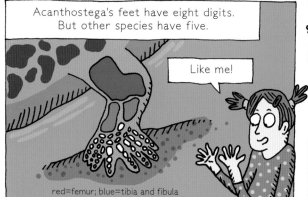

red=femur; blue=tibia and fibula

One of these five-fingered amphibians is the common ancestor of all the reptiles, birds, and mammals today, and of course humans!

But there are also still species with lobed fins!

Eusthenopteron

Tiktaalik

Acanthostega

After 100 million years, plants have undergone tremendous evolution. During the **Carboniferous**, huge forests cover the plains!

Lepidodendrons 100 feet (30 meters) tall and **tree ferns** rise above an understory of horsetails and **Sigillaria**.

It's a world of green and brown, without a trace of red or yellow, because **flowers** have not yet appeared.

The insects are now numerous . . . and often huge!

Cockroaches feed on debris, and **dragonflies** are carnivores.

As for the millipede **Arthropleura**, it may be a vegetarian!

Their giant size could be linked to the composition of the atmosphere, which is very rich in oxygen.

When the plants die, they are buried in the mud of the marsh and others take their place. As they accumulate underground, they will slowly turn into coal.

The Carboniferous is the age of coal . . .

. . . and also the age of roaches!

The first **terrestrial vertebrates** live like today's amphibians. They lay their eggs in the water, even the ones that move about and hunt on dry land.

Whatever the adults' lifestyle, their **larvae** are aquatic.

Cacops, terrestrial lifestyle

Diplocaulus, aquatic lifestyle

amphibian larva

Limnoscelis

Some of their cousins, the **reptiliomorphs**, look like reptiles.

Among all these animals, one line is responsible for an extraordinary innovation: the **amniotic egg**.

This egg is surrounded by an impermeable shell that keeps it from drying out.

The embryo is contained in a pocket, the amnion. It draws its nourishment from another pocket, the yolk sac.

The yolk sac is the yellow of a chicken's egg!

shell

yolk sac

The first **amniotes** resemble lizards. They no longer depend on finding water holes in order to reproduce.

They will soon give rise to two distinct groups:

Ophiacodon (10 ft / 3 m)

Petrolacosaurus (16 in / 40 cm)

the **sauropsids**, which are the ancestors of all reptiles and birds . . .

and the **synapsids**, which give rise to the mammals.

At the end of the Paleozoic, the planet witnesses the appearance of heavily armored giants.

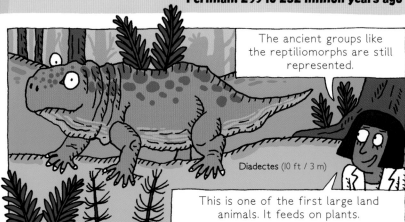

The ancient groups like the reptiliomorphs are still represented.

Diadectes (10 ft / 3 m)

This is one of the first large land animals. It feeds on plants.

Among the sauropsids, some species become enormous.

Scutosaurus (length 10 ft / 3 m, weight 1 ton)

It looks like a dinosaur!

No, it's a **pareiasaur**. With its splayed legs, it doesn't walk like the dinosaurs, which won't appear for another 60 million years.

The pareiasaurs live in herds. They're herbivores, and are protected by a shell of bony spikes.

Do all the animals become giants?

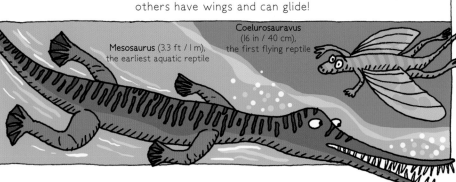

No, small animals still are more numerous and varied. The fauna diversifies in all directions. Some small reptiles adapt to the aquatic environment, while others have wings and can glide!

Mesosaurus (3.3 ft / 1 m), the earliest aquatic reptile

Coelurosauravus (16 in / 40 cm), the first flying reptile

REPTILES UNLIKE THE OTHERS

Among the first synapsids, several species have a dorsal sail supported by extensions of the vertebrae.

Dimetrodon (13 ft / 4 m), one of the largest carnivores of its time

The sail may have let them regulate their internal temperature by orienting themselves relative to the sun. It may also have helped attract a mate.

Like a **peacock**'s tail!

In the middle of the Permian, these reptiles are replaced by the **dinocephalians**.

Estemmenosuchus (10 ft / 3 m)

They have the massive body of an herbivore but the teeth of a carnivore.

And a funny-looking head!

Other dinocephalians, the **anteosaurs**, are entirely carnivorous.

Gorgonops (6.5 ft / 2 m)

The **gorgonopsians** have two long canine teeth like those of a saber-toothed tiger.

Anteosaur (10 ft / 3 m)

Charassognathus (20 in / 50 cm)

At the end of the Permian a new group appears: the **cynodonts**. On their jaws they have **vibrissae**—long, sensitive hairs.

Like . . .

. . . a cat's whiskers! These "reptiles" were probably covered in fur!

The Paleozoic ends with a catastrophe of planetary dimensions in which 90 percent of the flora and fauna die!

Pareiasaurus

Gorgonops

Entire groups disappear: the trilobites, the placoderm fish, the pareiasaurs, the gorgonopsians . . .

It's the largest **extinction** in Earth's history.

Because the crisis stretches over several million years, we think it has multiple causes. Sea levels drop more than 800 feet (250 m), which greatly reduces the habitat of the coastal animals.

For hundreds of thousands of years, volcanoes in Siberia produce clouds of ash and toxic gases, which disturb the climate.

The oceans become very low in oxygen. In addition, marine microorganisms emit huge quantities of toxic **methane**.

In spite of everything, some animals survive, either because they are able to live with the changes or . . . just by chance!

The only species of **sea urchin** that escapes extinction will give rise to all of today's species!

Some cynodonts live through it, and eventually will give rise to the mammals.

250 million years ago, at the beginning of the Mesozoic, or Secondary era, the fauna is still not very diverse. **Lystrosaurus** makes up 90 percent of the terrestrial fauna.

There are also carnivores that prey on these vast herds.

Lystrosaurus
(3.3 ft / 1 m)

Garjainia (12 in / 30 cm)

Thrinaxodon
(20 in / 50 cm)

Procolophon
(12 in / 30 cm)

The crisis was catastrophic, but it left the field open for evolution.

New species will begin to appear, very different from the previous ones.

During the **Triassic**, **reptiles** dominate the world!

There's not much to dominate, since most species have disappeared!

One family of reptiles, the **archosaurs**, will become more and more important.

Proterosuchus walks like a crocodile. With its legs splayed to the sides, this predator is not very fast.

Proterosuchus (6.5 ft / 2 m)

They're not all carnivores. **Desmatosuchus** also looks like a croc, but it feeds on aquatic plants.

It's well protected!

It's hunted by bigger archosaurs like **Fasolasuchus**, which weighs several tons and is a good runner with long legs.

Desmatosuchus (16 ft / 5 m)

The end of the Triassic is another time of extinction. Most of the archosaurs disappear . . .

. . . but not all! Three lines survive: the **crocodiles**, the **pterosaurs**, and the **dinosaurs**.

Fasolasuchus (26 ft / 8 m)

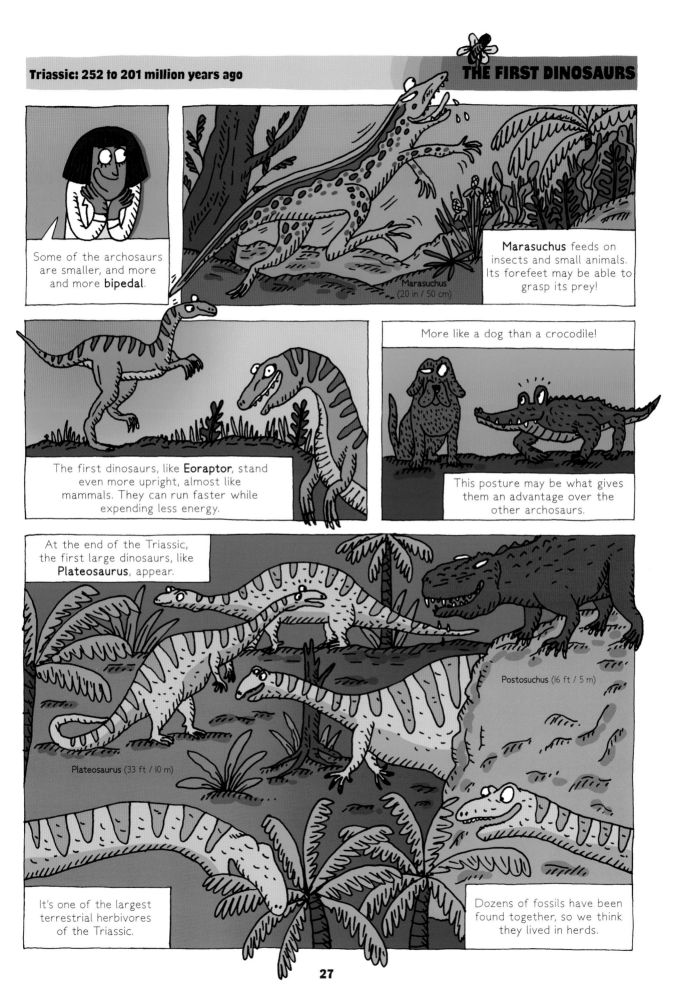

Some of the archosaurs are smaller, and more and more **bipedal**.

Marasuchus feeds on insects and small animals. Its forefeet may be able to grasp its prey!

Marasuchus (20 in / 50 cm)

The first dinosaurs, like **Eoraptor**, stand even more upright, almost like mammals. They can run faster while expending less energy.

More like a dog than a crocodile!

This posture may be what gives them an advantage over the other archosaurs.

At the end of the Triassic, the first large dinosaurs, like **Plateosaurus**, appear.

Postosuchus (16 ft / 5 m)

Plateosaurus (33 ft / 10 m)

It's one of the largest terrestrial herbivores of the Triassic.

Dozens of fossils have been found together, so we think they lived in herds.

During the Triassic, the **archosaurs** face competition from the **cynodonts**. They are carnivores too, but much smaller.

Yes, they eat insects and snails!

And there is an even more important difference: they are covered with hair, almost like mammals!

Cynognathus (3.3 ft / 1 m)

Cynognathus has a large head and the teeth of a predator. Its name means "dog jaw."

That's a funny-looking head for a dog!

Morganucodon (6 in / 15 cm)

It's not a dog! It's not even a mammal. Its feet are splayed wide apart, more like those of a reptile.

The world 230 million years ago

It has been found in the Americas and in Africa, which shows that those continents were joined at the time.

Toward the end of the Triassic, some cynodonts evolve and give rise to the first true mammals.

Morganucodon was covered with hair. We think it nursed its young. But it still laid eggs, like its ancestors.

And like **platypuses!**

Most of the first mammals were small carnivores that ate insects or worms, but they would soon diversify.

Castorocauda (16 in / 40 cm)

Castorocauda, which lived during the Jurassic, had a tail like a beaver and hunted fish underwater.

THE PTEROSAURS

The **pterosaurs** make their appearance. The air is filled with their raucous cries, and soon flying reptiles the size of airplanes darken the skies of the **Mesozoic Era**.

Eudimorphodon (3.3 ft / 1 m)

Yes, but we'll have to wait a while! During the Triassic, their wingspan doesn't exceed 6.5 feet (2 meters).

And we have no idea whether they made raucous cries!

Many pterosaurs eat fish.

The smallest ones eat insects.

young **Pteranodon** (wingspan 10-20 ft / 3-6 m)

Anurognathus (wingspan 20 in / 50 cm)

Pterodaustro (wingspan 4.3 ft / 1.3 m)

Pterodaustro's long, thin teeth let it filter marsh water to feed on plankton.

Sort of like a flamingo!

At the end of the Cretaceous, only large pterosaurs remain. **Quetzalcoatlus** doesn't have any teeth; it may be a scavenger.

Ooh, that one is really pretty!

Quetzalcoatlus (wingspan 33 ft / 10 m)

We don't actually know what color they were; these colors are made up!

There are, in fact, giant reptiles, but the marine fauna also includes lots of small animals!

Reefs form along the coastlines. They're not created by corals, but by large mollusks called **rudists**.

During the **Jurassic**, sea monsters invade the oceans!

Ammonites are much more diverse than during the Paleozoic. Some species live near the bottom, others in the open sea.

Some are only a few millimeters in diameter (less than ⅛ inch), while others reach 8 feet 2 (2.5 meters). These mollusks are carnivores.

It looks like an **octopus** with a shell!

The **belemnites**, cousins of the ammonites, resemble squids.

Ichthyosaurs are marine reptiles. They have to come to the surface to breathe, like cetaceans. They hunt fish and ammonites.

Plesiosaurs swim using legs that have transformed into paddles.

Pliosaurs resemble them, but their heads are much bigger and their necks are shorter. They are the largest marine predators of the Jurassic.

Shastasaurus (69 ft / 21 m)

Mosasaurus (60 ft / 18 m)

We know of nearly 500 species of fossil marine reptiles!

Elasmosaurus (46 ft / 14 m)

Pliosaurus (43 ft / 13 m)

And each family has its giants!

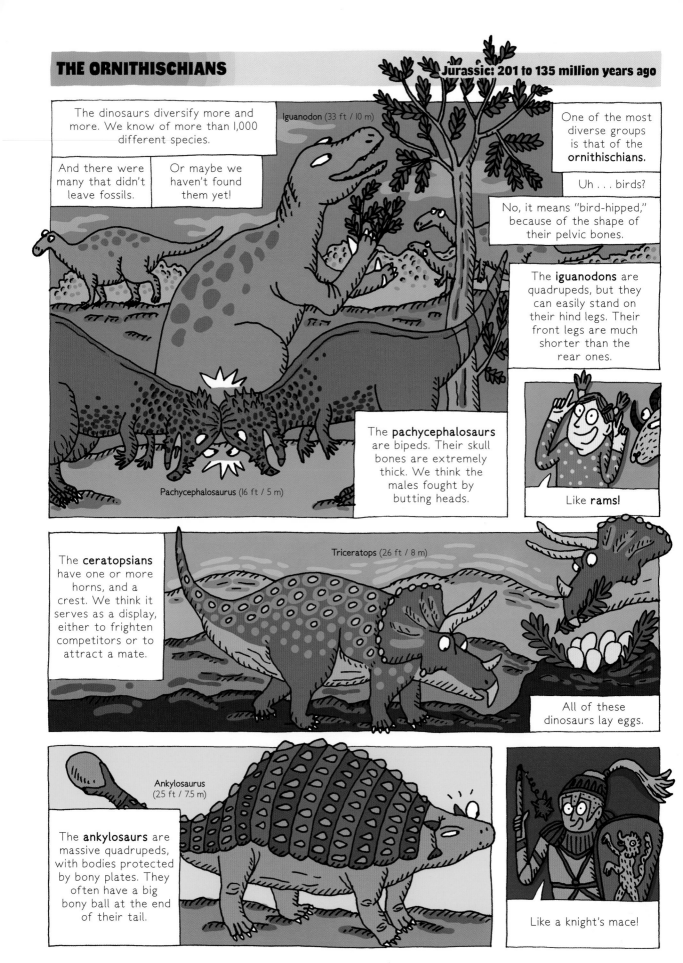

The dinosaurs diversify more and more. We know of more than 1,000 different species.

And there were many that didn't leave fossils.

Or maybe we haven't found them yet!

Iguanodon (33 ft / 10 m)

One of the most diverse groups is that of the **ornithischians.**

Uh . . . birds?

No, it means "bird-hipped," because of the shape of their pelvic bones.

The **iguanodons** are quadrupeds, but they can easily stand on their hind legs. Their front legs are much shorter than the rear ones.

The **pachycephalosaurs** are bipeds. Their skull bones are extremely thick. We think the males fought by butting heads.

Pachycephalosaurus (16 ft / 5 m)

Like **rams!**

The **ceratopsians** have one or more horns, and a crest. We think it serves as a display, either to frighten competitors or to attract a mate.

Triceratops (26 ft / 8 m)

All of these dinosaurs lay eggs.

Ankylosaurus (25 ft / 7.5 m)

The **ankylosaurs** are massive quadrupeds, with bodies protected by bony plates. They often have a big bony ball at the end of their tail.

Like a knight's mace!

Earth's crust is dragged apart by the movement of the molten rock several miles beneath our feet! The dinosaurs are carried along as if they're on rafts!

At the beginning of the Jurassic, **Pangaea**, the single continent, begins to break up.

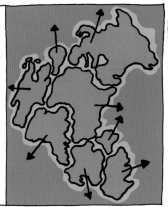

These rafts are huge, and very slow. They move an inch or so a year for millions of years.

So what happens to the dinosaurs?

They don't realize it, of course, but their evolution is going to be influenced by these movements.

The story of the stegosaurs begins with small bipedal herbivores like **Scutellosaurus**. Its skin is covered with small bony plates.

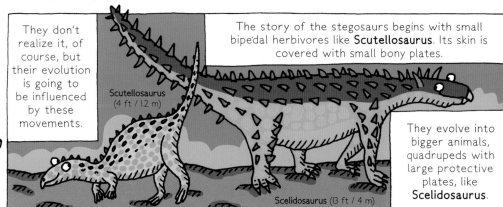

Scutellosaurus (4 ft / 1.2 m)

Scelidosaurus (13 ft / 4 m)

They evolve into bigger animals, quadrupeds with large protective plates, like **Scelidosaurus**.

And then the **stegosaurs**, which are much bigger, appear. But since the continents are separating, they will evolve differently from each other.

The stegosaurs, 150 million years ago

Are the stegosaurs the only ones that travel like that?

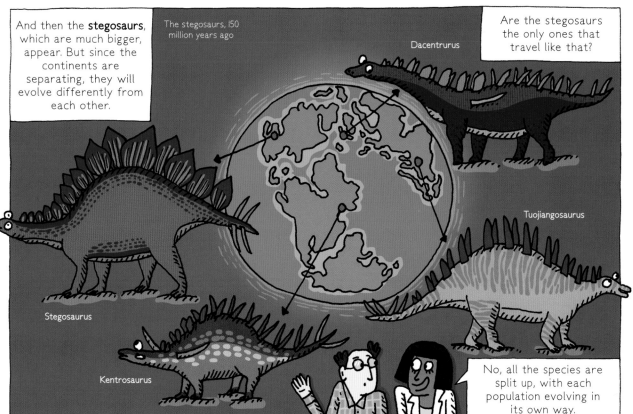

Dacentrurus

Tuojiangosaurus

Stegosaurus

Kentrosaurus

No, all the species are split up, with each population evolving in its own way.

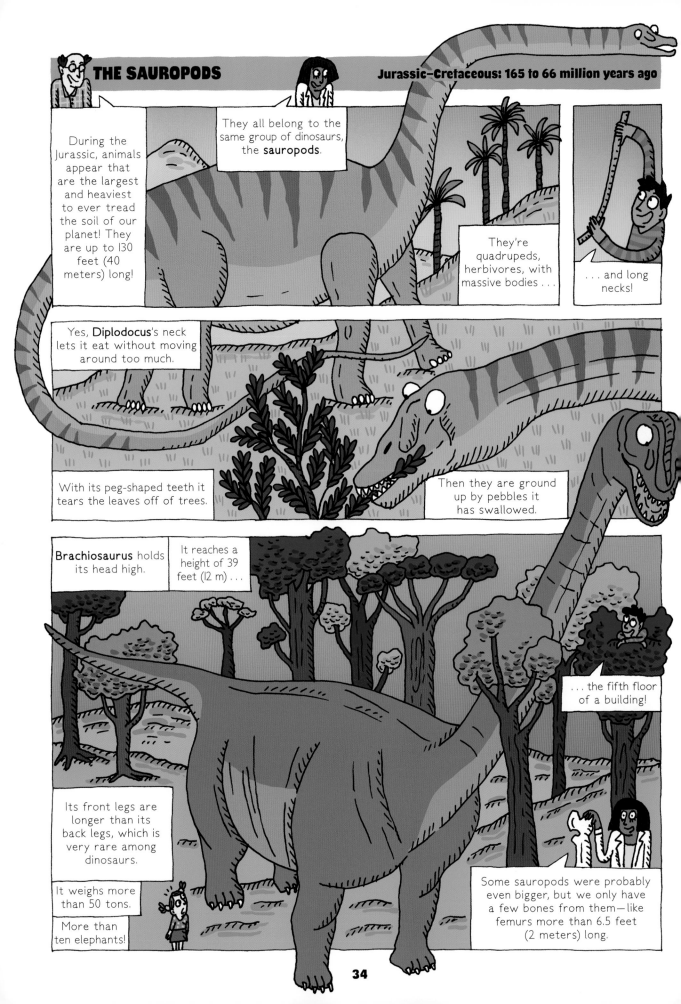

During the Jurassic, animals appear that are the largest and heaviest to ever tread the soil of our planet! They are up to 130 feet (40 meters) long!

They all belong to the same group of dinosaurs, the **sauropods**.

They're quadrupeds, herbivores, with massive bodies . . .

. . . and long necks!

Yes, **Diplodocus**'s neck lets it eat without moving around too much.

With its peg-shaped teeth it tears the leaves off of trees.

Then they are ground up by pebbles it has swallowed.

Brachiosaurus holds its head high.

It reaches a height of 39 feet (12 m) . . .

. . . the fifth floor of a building!

Its front legs are longer than its back legs, which is very rare among dinosaurs.

It weighs more than 50 tons.

More than ten elephants!

Some sauropods were probably even bigger, but we only have a few bones from them—like femurs more than 6.5 feet (2 meters) long.

34

The dinosaurs that prey on these herbivores are themselves enormous!

The **theropods** are all bipeds, with powerful hind legs and small forelegs.

Ceratosaurus has two short horns on its snout.

Ceratosaurus (20 ft / 6 m)

It's a carnivore and probably also a scavenger, feeding on dead animals.

The **spinosaurs**, like **Baryonyx**, have less massive bodies and longer snouts adapted for catching fish.

Like crocodiles!

Carcharodontosaurus is one of the biggest theropods.

Its jaws are armed with 80 teeth, some of which are more than 8 inches (20 centimeters) long!

Carcharodontosaurus (46 ft / 14 m)

But why did these dinosaurs become so big?

The biggest sauropods had an advantage, perhaps because the carnivores were afraid of them. But the biggest predators also had an advantage, because they had more prey animals available. In the end, herbivores and carnivores evolved in the same direction.

Like an endless race!

At the end of the Jurassic, the sky is full of new flying creatures: birds!

We know now that they are the ancestors of birds, but at that time it was impossible to foresee!

They're dinosaurs . . . almost like the others. **Archaeopteryx** is one of the most ancient among them.

But it has feathers, so it's a bird!

It's not that simple! It has feathers and it flies. But it also has teeth, claws, and a dinosaur tail.

And its skeleton closely resembles those of other carnivorous dinosaurs.

Ah, that one is definitely a dinosaur.

Not so fast! Close cousins of the **tyrannosaurs** are covered with filaments like a sort of down.

Adult tyrannosaurs have a scaly skin, but their young may have rudimentary plumage.

And some of these feathered dinosaurs can fly—or at least glide, like **Microraptor**.

The **dromaeosaurids** have real feathers, even the large species.

That one's a **raptor**!

Yes, you can tell by its large, curved talons.

WINGS AND TEETH

The down and rudimentary feathers that most of these dinosaurs have do not enable them to fly.

Caudipteryx

This plumage has other functions, for example conserving body heat or attracting a mate during a courtship display.

Therizinosaurus

Many dinosaurs behave like birds: they lay eggs in a nest and incubate them until they hatch.

Oviraptor

Their feathers may help them keep the eggs warm.

And not break them when they sit on them!

Eventually some dinosaurs use their plumage to fly, especially the line that gives rise to birds.

Ichthyornis

Some of these toothed birds quickly evolve into swimmers, unable to fly!

Hesperornis

But others continue to become lighter, for example by losing their teeth.

So the birds of today are dinosaurs with feathers but no teeth!

In the rivers and marshes, **crocodiles** compete with the predatory dinosaurs.

Suchomimus (36 ft / 11 m)

Sarcosuchus (39 ft / 12 m)

Evolution never stops. Alongside the dinosaurs, new species are constantly appearing.

Sarcosuchus is perhaps the largest crocodile of all time!

The legs of some other reptiles, related to lizards, become smaller and smaller.

Tetrapodophis is a four-legged snake!

Tetrapodophis (8 in / 20 cm)

Pythons still have small leg bones under the skin.

And very quickly, snakes evolve. They become venomous, or very large, or very small. . . .

Sanajeh (11.5 ft / 3.5 m)

Sanajeh eats small dinosaurs.

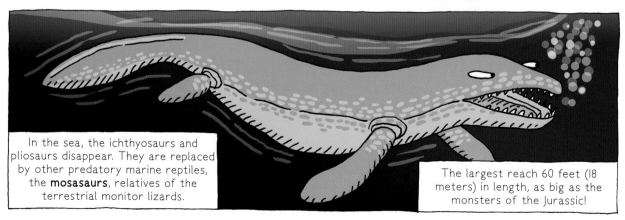

In the sea, the ichthyosaurs and pliosaurs disappear. They are replaced by other predatory marine reptiles, the **mosasaurs**, relatives of the terrestrial monitor lizards.

The largest reach 60 feet (18 meters) in length, as big as the monsters of the Jurassic!

FUR BALLS

Meanwhile, the **mammals** are biding their time.

During the Cretaceous the mammals are numerous, but they don't have any expectations.

They're just trying to avoid predators.

Most of them no longer lay eggs, but instead carry their young until birth.

Sinodelphys
(6 in / 15 cm)

The first **marsupials** appear. As with kangaroos, the young develop in their mother's front pouch.

Eomaia (4 in / 10 cm)

Among the placental mammals, the young are nourished by the placenta until birth.

Many lead a nocturnal life, which lets them go about unnoticed.

Most of them eat insects and worms.

Others are herbivores, like the **multituberculates.**

Sinobataar
(6 in / 15 cm)

This family disappears without descendants about 35 million years ago.

Not all the mammals are tiny. **Repenomamus** is the size of a large badger.

Repenomamus (3.3 ft / 1 m)

The bones of a small dinosaur it had eaten were found inside its fossil skeleton!

FLOWERS FOR THE DINOSAURS

During the **Cretaceous**, the forests are abloom with flowers. Fragrant roses and pretty daisies at last!

That didn't happen in the blink of an eye! And the first flowers are very plain.

Jurassic landscapes are uniformly green, dominated by ferns and conifers.

Some insects feed on pollen. The plants benefit, because the insects carry pollen from plant to plant and help them reproduce.

Plants begin to produce nectar, which attracts insects. They also develop flowers, which signal their location.

For their part, insects specialize in transporting pollen.

The insects are attracted by the colors and fragrances of the flowers!

The flowering plants and the insects develop alongside one another.

Yes, they need each other and they evolve together. This is what we call **coevolution**.

More and more, the forests resemble those of today.

With dinosaurs as a bonus!

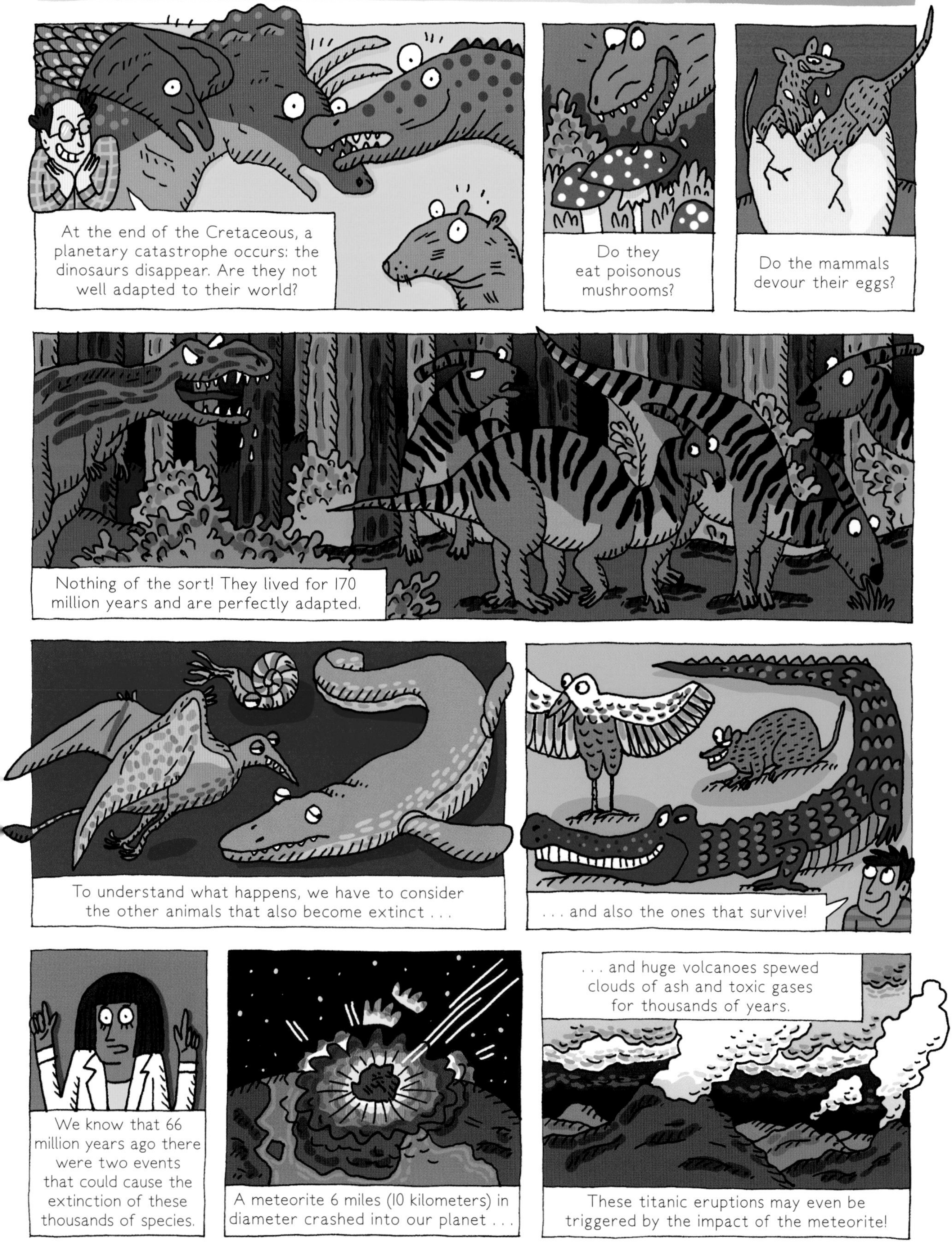
At the end of the Cretaceous, a planetary catastrophe occurs: the dinosaurs disappear. Are they not well adapted to their world?
Do they eat poisonous mushrooms?
Do the mammals devour their eggs?
Nothing of the sort! They lived for 170 million years and are perfectly adapted.
To understand what happens, we have to consider the other animals that also become extinct . . .
. . . and also the ones that survive!
We know that 66 million years ago there were two events that could cause the extinction of these thousands of species.
A meteorite 6 miles (10 kilometers) in diameter crashed into our planet . . .
. . . and huge volcanoes spewed clouds of ash and toxic gases for thousands of years.
These titanic eruptions may even be triggered by the impact of the meteorite!

Ash from the explosion of the meteorite and from the volcanoes darkens the sky and upsets the world's climate.

That causes the death of a large portion of the vegetation.

The **large herbivores** starved . . .

. . . then the large predators, which could no longer find prey.

But how did other animals survive?

Actually, many of them died too. But the **crocodiles**, the **turtles**, and the **fish** may have been less affected because of their aquatic lifestyle.

The **birds** may have been better able to adapt because of their small size.

As for the **small mammals**, they may have been used to surviving difficult periods by going into a resting state in their burrows.

That's a lot of "may have beens"!

There's still a lot we don't understand about this event!

THE CENOZOIC
66 million years ago

After the terrible catastrophe at the end of the Cretaceous, most of the large animals have disappeared, but some mammals have survived. Vegetation is abundant, and there are fewer predators.

In a few million years, the mammals' evolution will produce species that are much more numerous and diverse than during all of the preceding eras.

Titanoides (length 10 ft / 3 m)

Gastornis (height 6.5 ft / 2 m)

Phenacodus (length 5 ft / 1.5 m)

Dissacus (length 4.3 ft / 1.3 m)

Chriacus (length 3.3 ft / 1 m)

Ptilodus (length 12-20 in / 30-50 cm)

At first they are ground-dwellers or tree-climbers, but they rapidly occupy all the habitats left open by the extinction of the dinosaurs.

Birds, too, take advantage of the changes; giant flightless species appear.

The dinosaurs had prevented the mammals from evolving, but now there's a veritable explosion!

Vegetation is abundant, which makes possible the appearance of all sorts of new species, small and large.

Mammals occupy the wetlands, a particularly rich habitat.

Coryphodon
(length 8 ft / 2.5 m)

Coryphodon has an amphibious lifestyle, similar to that of a hippopotamus.

Uintatherium
(length 13 ft / 4 m)

Uintatherium is one of the largest animals of the early Eocene. It weighs more than 2 tons!

Its head is really bizarre!

Maybe it is attractive to females!

Herbivorores and carnivores begin to appear side by side.

Mesonyx preys on small animals, probably as a solitary hunter.

It looks like a wolf!

Mesonyx
(length 5 ft / 1.5 m)

Phenacodus
(length 5 ft / 1.5 m)

With its big feet, it doesn't run very fast. And it doesn't have claws, it has small hooves!

One of its cousins, **Andrewsarchus**, is among the biggest carnivores in Earth's history; its skull alone measures 3 feet (90 centimeters)!

Andrewsarchus
(length 13 ft / 4 m)

It's really an omnivore, mostly a scavenger.

During the Eocene, the world becomes warmer and wetter. Vast forests cover the continents.

Their flowers and fruits are eaten by numerous climbing species.

Carpolestes
(6 in / 15 cm)

Carpolestes is a very small herbivore, hardly bigger than a mouse. But unlike a rodent, it has opposable thumbs, and nails rather than claws. It's a **plesiadapiform**, related to the first monkeys.

Also living in the trees are its cousins, like **Darwinius**.

Its eyes face forward, which gives it better vision.

Darwinius
(23 in / 58 cm)

It looks like a **lemur**!

Yes, but it has a nose like a dog's, not like a monkey's! This is the group that will give rise to the **lemurs** and the **monkeys**.

Icaronycteris
(wingspan 15 in / 37 cm)

This is also the time of the first **bats**.

Planetetherium
(length 10 in / 25 cm)

Planetetherium can glide from tree to tree using "sails" of skin stretched between its legs.

And all of these little animals attract carnivores.

Yes, like **Miacis**! It's the size of a marten, and a good climber. It's one of the first true carnivores.

Miacis
(12 in / 30 cm)

Its family will give rise to two lines. One leads to the wolves, bears, and seals; the other, to the hyenas and felines.

Eohippus is the size of a dog. It is the precursor of the horses, zebras, and donkeys.

Heptodon is closer to the tapirs.

One group of animals will dominate the grasslands for millions of years.

Hyrachyus is one of the oldest rhinoceroses.

Eotitanops is an ancestor of the massive Megacerops.

They are very similar, but their lines are going to diverge. They all have an uneven number of toes, from which they get the name **perissodactyls**.

From the Greek *perissos*, "uneven-numbered," and *dactylos*, "finger"!

Miohippus (24 million years ago)

Mesohippus (35 million years ago)

Merychippus (15 million years ago)

The **Eohippus** group will give rise to hundreds of species of horses.

Merychippus is one of the biggest, the size of a sheep! It's one of the first horses to eat only grass.

Each of its feet has three toes.

Today, only a few of these magnificent animals remain. What a shame!

It's true, they were replaced by the **ruminants**.

Small mammals are still the most numerous, but evolution also produces some very large species.

Since the time of the dinosaurs, Earth has not been home to any more giants. They're finally beginning to reappear!

Paraceratherium is probably the biggest mammal in the history of Earth. Although it doesn't have a horn, it belongs to the rhinoceros family.

It's also called **Indricotherium** or **Baluchitherium**.

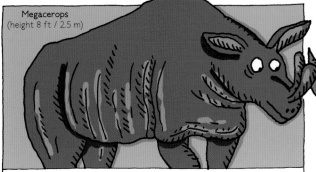

Megacerops (height 8 ft / 2.5 m)

Megacerops is descended from the little **Eotitanops**, so it's related to horses and rhinoceroses.

Arsinoitherium (height 5.5 ft / 1.7 m)

Arsinoitherium has the lifestyle of a rhinoceros.

entelodont (height 6 ft / 1.8 m)

An **entelodont** resembles a giant wild boar. It eats anything it can find. It's very fast, and can chase down small prey.

The **chalicotheres** are cousins of the horses, but their hooves have evolved into claws!

It's a gorilla-horse!

47

The Eocene witnesses the beginning of one of evolution's most extraordinary stories—that of the **whales**!

We can begin the story with **Indohyus**, a small herbivore that lived 50 million years ago. It's the size of a house cat and has small hooves.

But that's nothing like a whale!

True, but some of its bones and its teeth resemble those of the future whales.

Indohyus may have been the ancestor of a slightly larger animal, **Pakicetus.**

It probably has an amphibious lifestyle. It catches fish for food.

Like an otter!

Pakicetus, or a related species, evolves and gives rise to **Ambulocetus**, which is even bigger and spends its life in the water.

Ambulocetus swims very well, and hunts sort of like a crocodile.

It has webbed feet!

Its skull closely resembles those of prehistoric whales, which will appear a few million years later.

Ambulocetus could be the ancestor of the cetaceans.

Ambulocetus means "walking whale"!

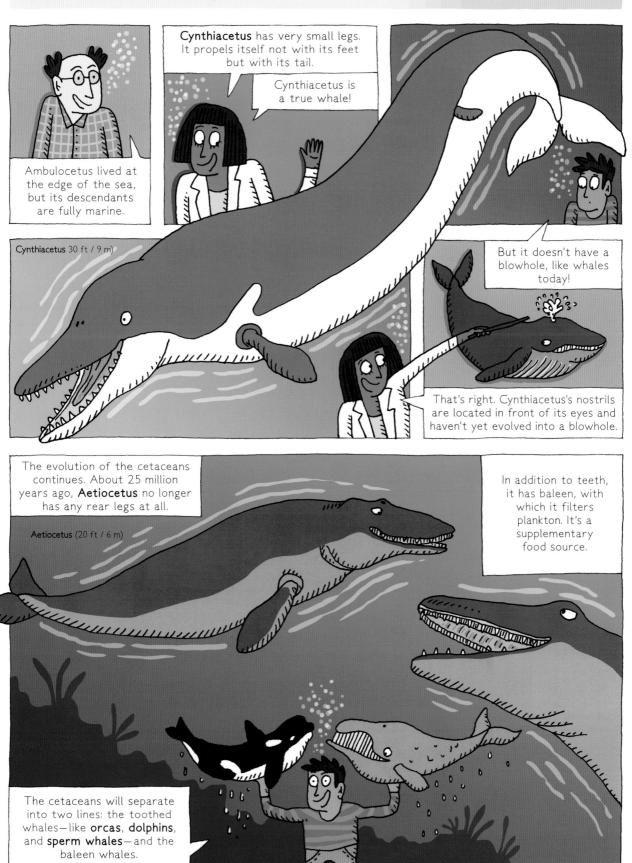

Ambulocetus lived at the edge of the sea, but its descendants are fully marine.

Cynthiacetus has very small legs. It propels itself not with its feet but with its tail.

Cynthiacetus is a true whale!

Cynthiacetus 30 ft / 9 m)

But it doesn't have a blowhole, like whales today!

That's right. Cynthiacetus's nostrils are located in front of its eyes and haven't yet evolved into a blowhole.

The evolution of the cetaceans continues. About 25 million years ago, **Aetiocetus** no longer has any rear legs at all.

Aetiocetus (20 ft / 6 m)

In addition to teeth, it has baleen, with which it filters plankton. It's a supplementary food source.

The cetaceans will separate into two lines: the toothed whales—like **orcas, dolphins,** and **sperm whales**—and the baleen whales.

It's also during the Eocene that an astonishing organ, the **elephant**'s trunk, appears!

At the time, there was no way to foresee what **Numidotherium**'s descendants would become.

Numidotherium
(height 3.3 ft / 1 m)

It was only one of many species of African mammals with a more or less aquatic lifestyle!

Its upper jaw carried large tusk-like incisors.

Its nose and upper lip were fused into a short trunk.

Like a tapir's!

These animals evolved into more massive species, like **Phiomia**.

Phiomia
(height 8 ft / 2.5 m)

Its heavy tusks weighed down its head. Its neck muscles strengthened.

The shortening of its neck was compensated for by a lengthening of its trunk.

That's practical for elephants with their long legs!

This family diversified more and more.

Deinotherium had tusks that point downward.

With its flattened tusks, **Platybelodon** could pull up aquatic plants.

Platybelodon
(height 7 ft / 2.2 m)

This line will give rise to the elephants and mammoths.

There are 180 known fossil species. Only two remain: the African and Asian elephants.

Ever since the Jurassic, South America has been a raft drifting away from the other continents.

It's more like an island! It remains close to North America, but the Atlantic Ocean widens, and little by little it moves away from Africa.

South America

The animals will evolve in their own ways.

Africa

Thoatherium (height 28 in / 70 cm)

The mammals that survived the crisis at the end of the Cretaceous give rise to hoofed herbivores like the **litopterns** and the **astrapotheres**.

Astrapotherium (height 3.3 ft / 1 m)

There are also carnivores, like **Thylacosmilus**.

It's a saber-toothed tiger!

It's a **marsupial tiger**, more closely related to kangaroos than to "real" tigers!

Phorusrhacos (height 8 ft / 2.5 m)

Another large predator is **Phorusrhacos**.

As always, there are carnivores and herbivores.

The species are different, but the food chains are the same!

While the Atlantic is still narrow, animals cross the ocean and reach South America.

By swimming?

No, on trees uprooted by storms. That's probably how monkeys come from Africa . . .

. . . and rodents from North America.

They, too, evolve into new species: **Phoberomys** is a rodent that weighs half a ton!

A new group becomes more and more important: the ruminants.

During the **Miocene**, Earth's climate becomes colder and drier. Grasslands and savannahs replace the forests.

Archaeomeryx, one of the first, lived during the Eocene 40 million years ago.

Archaeomeryx (height 10 in / 25 cm)

It resembles a **musk deer,** the smallest ruminant today.

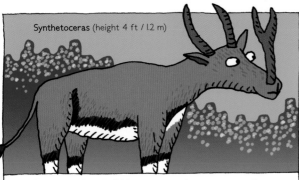

Synthetoceras (height 4 ft / 1.2 m)

Thousands of different species appear, often with antlers or horns.

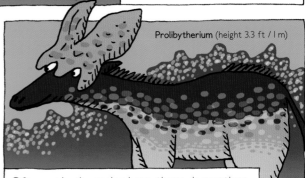

Prolibytherium (height 3.3 ft / 1 m)

Often, only the males have these decorations. They use them to vie with other males for the attention of females.

Some males, like **Hoplitomeryx**, also have long canine teeth.

It lived 8 million years ago on an island in the Mediterranean.

Garganoaetus (height 3.3 ft / 1 m)

Both sexes have horns, which may protect them from **Garganoaetus**, a giant eagle.

But not from **crocodiles!**

All the ruminants have two or four toes.

They're **artiodactyls.**

From the Greek *artios*, "even-numbered," and *dactylos*, "finger"!

Ampelomeryx, the giraffe-deer

But most importantly, they can easily digest grass, thanks to their special stomach with several compartments.

The **giraffe**'s neck is one of the most famous stories of evolution: how did giraffes attain their prodigious height?

I think they wanted to reach the leaves on the highest branches. As a result of the stretching, their necks got longer! It's simple!

It may be simple, but it's wrong! That's not how animals evolve.

First we need to look at what really happened.

Canthumeryx (height 3.3 ft / 1 m)

Sixteen million years ago, **Canthumeryx** was a small leaf-eater that lived in the African forests.

Samotherium (height 8 ft / 2.5 m)

Its descendants had longer necks, like **Samotherium**, 7 million years ago.

If the longer neck gave them an advantage, they passed that characteristic on to their young. And their necks got longer from generation to generation.

But what could the advantage have been? Maybe the ability to reach branches that others couldn't.

Maybe it also gave them a better weapon! During the mating season, male giraffes fight with their necks.

A neck-and-neck battle!

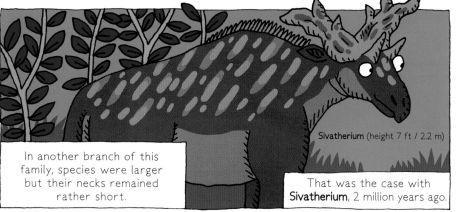

Sivatherium (height 7 ft / 2.2 m)

In another branch of this family, species were larger but their necks remained rather short.

That was the case with **Sivatherium**, 2 million years ago.

That line also produced today's **okapis**!

The Miocene ocean is one of the most dangerous in prehistory!

Yes, it's home to some of the biggest marine predators in the history of Earth.

The **megalodon** is a giant shark that can reach 60 feet (18 meters) in length.

In fact, all we have are its teeth! To estimate its size, we compare them with the teeth of today's **great white shark**.

Which is only 20 feet (6 meters) long!

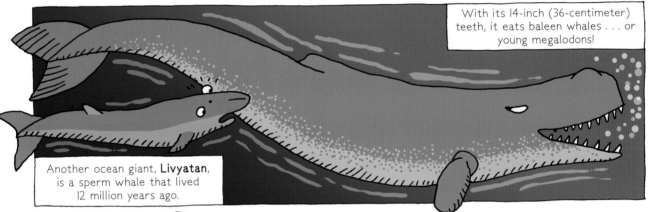

With its 14-inch (36-centimeter) teeth, it eats baleen whales . . . or young megalodons!

Another ocean giant, **Livyatan**, is a sperm whale that lived 12 million years ago.

During the Miocene, another family of carnivores turns toward the marine environment: the **seals** and **sea lions**.

Puijila (3.6 ft / 1.1 m)

Puijila is one of the oldest seals. Its webbed feet allow it to swim as well as to walk on land.

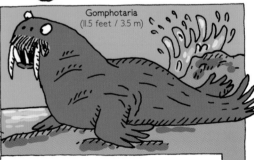

Gomphotaria (11.5 feet / 3.5 m)

Gomphotaria, an archaic walrus of 6 million years ago, is armed with two pairs of tusks.

Toothed birds reemerge from an earlier age and sow terror.

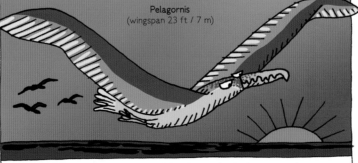

Pelagornis (wingspan 23 ft / 7 m)

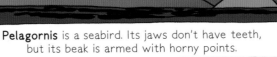

Pelagornis is a seabird. Its jaws don't have teeth, but its beak is armed with horny points.

It's twice the size of today's biggest birds, so it must have been scary anyway!

Like during the time of the dinosaurs, animals of the **Cenozoic** were faced with fierce predators!

At the beginning of this period, the principal carnivores were creodonts, like **Machaeroides**, which was the size of an otter . . .

. . . or **Hyaenodon**, which was much bigger. The related **Megistotherium** weighed as much as half a ton!

Hyaenodon
(height 4 ft / 1.2 m)

Little by little the creodonts were replaced by the carnivorans, the ancestors of today's carnivores.

The creodonts became extinct because they were weaker and less ferocious!

We don't know why they disappeared. Smaller brains? Less supple joints? Nevertheless, they lived for more than 50 million years!

Dissopsalis, one of the last creodonts

Amphicyon (height 4 ft / 1.2 m)

The carnivores split into two lines: the **caniforms**, including the dogs, the bears, and the **amphicyonids**, or "bear-dogs," which today have disappeared . . .

. . . and the **feliforms**, the first felines, like **Proailurus**, which was the size of a house cat.

Then came the saber-toothed tigers, like **Machairodus**.

Our ancestors came into contact with them, probably to their regret!

Machairodus
(height 4 ft / 1.2 m)

Finally we come to the pinnacle of evolution, the first humans!

They aren't the pinnacle! The first hominids are large monkeys like the others. And nothing foretells that they will be our ancestors!

Proconsul
(weight 40 lb / 18 kg)

The first hominoids, like **Proconsul**, lived in Africa between 20 million and 11 million years ago.

They eat fruits and leaves. The largest of them are the size of a **gorilla**.

Pierolapithecus
(height 4 ft / 1.2 m)

Then other large monkeys occupy Europe and Asia, like **Pierolapithecus**, which is found in Catalonia.

Sivapithecus
(height 5 ft / 1.5 m)

Sivapithecus, in India, is related to today's orangutan.

But it is in Africa that the hominids flourish.

Sahelanthropus
(7 million years ago)

Sahelanthropus, also called **Toumaï**, probably walks upright and not on all fours.

That is also the case with **Ardipithecus**, which lived 4.4 million years ago.

Ardipithecus

Three million years ago, several species of hominids occupied the African savannahs, like . . .

. . . **Paranthropes**, which ate mostly roots, leaves, and fruits . . .

. . . and **Australopithecus**, which also caught insects and other small animals. The famous Lucy was one of them!

And among them were our ancestors!

THE QUATERNARY

Pleistocene: 2.6 million to 12,000 years ago

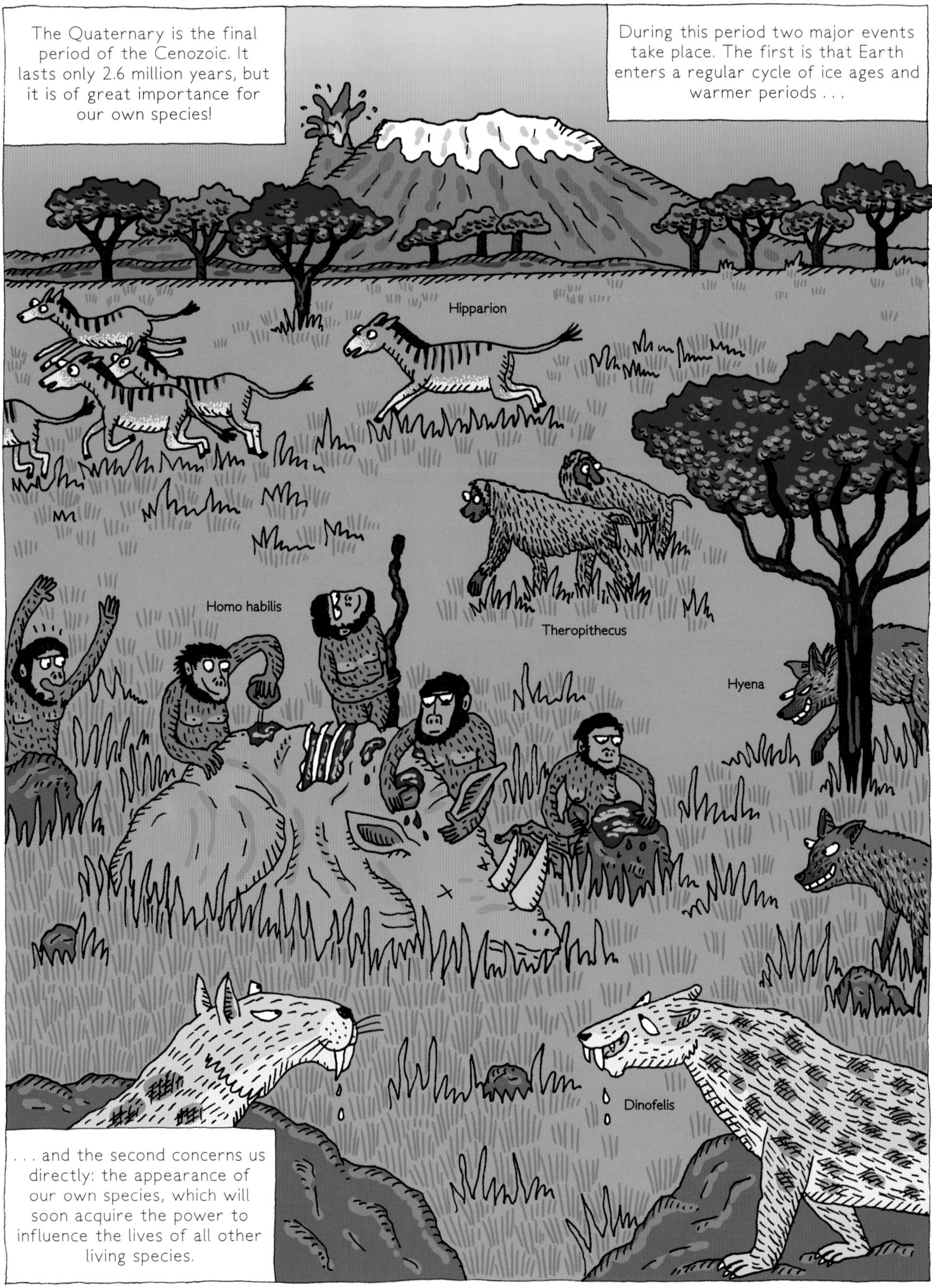

The Quaternary is the final period of the Cenozoic. It lasts only 2.6 million years, but it is of great importance for our own species!
During this period two major events take place. The first is that Earth enters a regular cycle of ice ages and warmer periods . . .
Hipparion
Homo habilis
Theropithecus
Hyena
Dinofelis
. . . and the second concerns us directly: the appearance of our own species, which will soon acquire the power to influence the lives of all other living species.

During the Quaternary, our planet experiences fluctuating temperatures, passing regularly from the oven to the freezer.

Yes, Earth alternates between periods of ice ages and thaws because of variations in its orbit around the sun.

When Earth receives less heat, the average temperature drops and glaciers invade the continents.

When it receives more heat, the glaciers recede and the climate becomes warmer and wetter.

During the last interglacial period, 120,000 years ago, hippopotamuses swam in the River Thames in England.

During glacial periods, part of the oceans' water is trapped in glaciers that cover as much as a third of the continents.

Sea levels drop by more than 300 feet (100 meters).

The English Channel no longer exists; it's replaced by a large river running into the Atlantic.

All the prehistory of mankind will be marked by the effects of the Ice Age.

So will the evolution of animals. During cold periods, they move into regions . . .

. . . that become islands during warm periods. They then evolve apart from the others.

Forests can't survive the climate of glacial periods. They give way to tall-grass steppes and to tundra, open prairies of mosses and lichens.

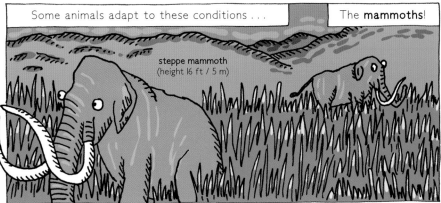

Some animals adapt to these conditions . . .

The **mammoths**!

steppe mammoth
(height 16 ft / 5 m)

They're not alone! Huge rhinoceroses like **Elasmotherium** live in Europe.

Elasmotherium
(height 6.5 ft / 2 m)

It weighs 4 metric tons and its horn is more than 5 feet (1.5 meters) long!

These giant species conserve heat more easily than small animals, so they have an advantage during glaciations.

Megaloceros is a giant deer.

Megaloceros
(height 6.5 ft / 2 m)

Its antlers weigh as much as 90 pounds (40 kilograms)!

The **cave bear** is one of the largest bears of prehistory, but it's mostly an herbivore.

The tundra is home to herds of **reindeer** . . . as well as predators.

Homotherium
(height 3.6 ft / 1.1 m)

reindeer
(height 4.3 ft / 1.3 m)

cave hyena
(height 3.3 ft / 1 m)

Hyenas in the snow? The world has turned upside down!

For millions of years South America evolves peacefully, apart from the rest of the world. Then suddenly volcanoes emerge from the ocean and reconnect it to North America!

That happens about 3 million years ago. Animals very quickly take advantage of this land bridge.

Megatheriums (huge ground sloths) and **glyptodons** (giant armadillos) move north, followed by numerous small animals.

At the same time, animals from the north move in the opposite direction.

The northern species are used to competing with the faunas of other continents, but the southern ones can't withstand this massive influx.

The giant predatory birds, deprived of their prey by the new carnivores, end up becoming extinct.

The **litopterns** are driven from their grasslands by llamas and other herbivores from the north.

The last of them, **Macrauchenia**, survives until 10,000 years ago.

And today, nothing remains of the ancient fauna of South America except the **opossums**, the **sloths**, the **anteaters**, and the **armadillos**!

For more than 50 million years Australia drifts, separating from the other continents. During the **Pleistocene**, its fauna is still isolated.

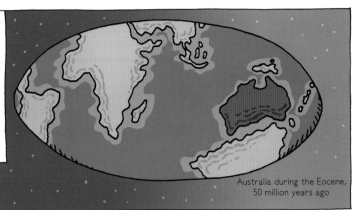

Before it separates, it is already populated by insects, reptiles, birds, and marsupials, the ancestors of almost all Australian mammals.

Australia during the Eocene, 50 million years ago

Kangaroos appear about 5 million years ago. **Procoptodon** is one of the largest.

Procoptodon
(height 6.5 ft / 2 m)

Palorchestes is like a tapir with claws.

Palorchestes
(height 3.9 ft / 1.2 m)

These herbivores play the same role as horses and antelopes on other continents.

Diprotodon, the largest marsupial ever known, eats bushes and grass.

Diprotodon
(height 6.9 ft / 2.1 m)

Among the marsupials there are also carnivorous species, like **Thylacoleo**.

Thylacoleo
(height 30 in / 75 cm)

Other predators, like the giant monitor lizard **Megalania**, compete with it for prey.

It looks like a **Komodo dragon** . . .

. . . but much bigger!

THE FIRST HUMANS

In the large family of hominids there suddenly appears a new species, completely different from the others . . . our ancestor!

We don't really know what distinguishes him from the others. He may be a little more curious, a little more sociable, a little more skillful with his hands; he is *Homo habilis*!

He lives in East Africa, in a savannah environment, where he eats plants and meat.

He's a hunter!

Maybe not yet, but he probably uses stone tools to slice up animals killed by the big carnivores.

Very soon another species appears, taller, with a bigger brain and able to move about easily on two legs. He is *Homo erectus*, erect man.

He's a hunter!

And he fashions more complex stone tools.

These early humans are the first to tame a basic element, fire!

Now they can cook their food, keep themselves warm at night, and protect themselves from wild animals.

We don't know whether they converse the way we do, but they certainly communicate among themselves to hunt, to build their huts . . .

. . . or to tell stories!

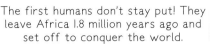

The first humans don't stay put! They leave Africa 1.8 million years ago and set off to conquer the world.

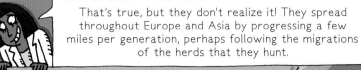

That's true, but they don't realize it! They spread throughout Europe and Asia by progressing a few miles per generation, perhaps following the migrations of the herds that they hunt.

In ten thousand generations you can cover some distance!

Some groups settle down, like the **Neanderthals** in Europe and part of Asia, but they continue to evolve.

Their brains are bigger than those of their ancestors. They're very adept at making tools.

They're excellent hunters!

Because they evolved separately, they are a little different from other humans . . . our own ancestors!

Pleistocene: 2.6 million to 12,000 years ago

Variations in sea level create new islands, where species evolve in unique ways. Islands are the playgrounds of evolution!

Sometimes food is scarcer on islands, but there often are no large predators, which is a great advantage.

On islands in the Mediterranean, **elephants** become smaller and smaller.

They shrink?

No, it's a change that takes place over many generations.

In the beginning, the biggest elephants have a hard time finding food. On the other hand, the smaller ones can feed themselves easily.

And since there's no risk of being eaten by big cats, their small size is not a problem!

They were barely the size of a big dog!

In each generation the smallest ones have a real advantage, to the point that evolution results in dwarf elephants.

On other islands, it was **hippopotamuses** or **deer** that became tiny.

At last we have reached the pinnacle of evolution, the king of nature . . . in other words, me! Well, not just me, modern man in general . . . *Homo sapiens*!

He's neither a king nor a pinnacle! But he's a skillful artisan and a very good hunter.

He's called **Cro-Magnon** because in 1868 some skeletons are found in a rock shelter at Cro-Magnon in France.

He, too, appears in Africa, about 150,000 years ago, and like his ancestors, he begins to travel the world.

He goes even farther than they did, reaching America and Australia.

These new people encounter the descendants of the first humans, but rarely mix with them. And all the others eventually die out.

If they had survived, today there would be several species of humans!

These are probably the first people to paint and carve on cliffs and cave walls.

paintings in Chauvet Cave

Thirty thousand years ago they were as gifted as we are!

Our bodies and brains have hardly changed at all in 50,000 years.

Twenty thousand years ago the climate begins to warm. The glaciers recede and sea level rises. It is the end of the last Ice Age!

It will still be cold for a few thousand years! But the warming was spectacular. Twelve thousand years ago it was warmer than it is today.

That must have been nice for the humans!

But not all the animals can adapt to these new conditions.

Forests replace the steppes. The **mammoths** and **rhinoceroses** can no longer find grass to eat.

On the other hand, the **deer**, the **elands**, and the **wild boars** adapt to life in the forest.

Little by little, the large fauna of the Ice Ages die off. It's also possible that humans contribute to this wave of extinctions!

In America it's the **mastodons**, the **giant sloths**, and the **horses** that disappear.

In Oceania, the **giant birds** that live on the islands disappear when humans arrive!

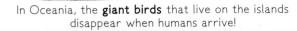

moa (height 10 ft / 3 m)

Little by little, humans abandon their way of life as nomadic hunters. They build houses, then villages.

They begin to cultivate the soil and to raise animals. That happens almost everywhere, but not at the same time.

And everywhere, the living world will be disrupted by human activity.

67

THE AGRICULTURAL REVOLUTION

Until this time, humans have been at the mercy of wild nature. Ten thousand years ago, they set out to tame it.

Actually, until this time they have lived in balance with nature.

But the lush environment, rich in natural resources, allows them to settle down and build houses.

To live more comfortably!

Before, they cultivated plants when they stopped somewhere for a few months. Now they clear large areas and sow grain.

With their harvests they can feed a rapidly growing population.

But that takes more work!

Because they're no longer nomadic, they make pottery vessels to store their harvests in.

They need wood for the posts of their houses and for the pottery kilns.

When they exhaust an area's natural resources, they build new villages a little farther along.

During the **Neolithic**, humans clear a large part of the forests of the Mediterranean.

It is said that one day a new animal arrived in a village, an animal that would become man's best friend: the **dog**!

When it approached humans, it was not yet a **dog**, it was a **wolf**! The least aggressive and least timid wolves got used to the presence of people, and little by little became dogs.

Ten thousand years ago, the first villagers begin to raise **wild sheep** and **goats**.

It's easier than hunting them!

Maybe. In any case, those are animals that do fairly well in captivity and in association with humans.

Then they domesticate more dangerous animals like **aurochs** and **wild boars**.

With each generation they select the most docile, and soon they have **cows** and **pigs**!

It's selection, like with evolution!

In South America, people domesticate **llamas** and **guinea pigs**.

And in China, **water buffaloes** and **chickens**!

Ten thousand years later, the villages are transformed into cities. Humans build enormous machines that make everything they need. Electricity keeps them warm, provides light, and lets them communicate with one another.

Scientific and technological progress have indeed revolutionized humans' way of life, at least in the cities.

But these changes are accompanied by an equally enormous consumption of energy—first from wood, then coal, oil, and uranium.

Humans consume more and more and more raw materials, and discard more and more waste.

Natural environments are exploited to the point of complete destruction. Others are polluted so badly that no animal can live there any longer.

Call me Destructor!

Gases released into the atmosphere by transportation, heating, factories, and agriculture trap more and more solar radiation, which heats the atmosphere.

Human activity has changed the planet so much that our epoch is called the **Anthropocene**.

The Age of Man!

Unfortunately, coexistence between humans and animals has not always been perfect.

We can even call it disastrous! Many species have simply been eliminated.

dodo (17th century)

Rodrigues tortoise (18th century)

thylacine, Tasmanian wolf (1936)

And it's not over! It looks as if the **baiji**, a Chinese river dolphin, is functionally extinct. This freshwater dolphin has not been observed since 2004.

What happened to it?

We don't know exactly. Probably pollution of the river where it lived and destruction of its habitat.

It's not just the large animals. The Saint Helena **earwig** was declared extinct in 2014.

Other species are gravely threatened. African **elephants** are hunted by poachers for their ivory tusks.

Rhinoceroses are killed for their horns, which some people believe have medicinal properties.

But the horns are just keratin, the same as our fingernails!

The number of species that disappear every year is 100 to 1,000 times greater than before the industrial era.

This could be the sixth period of mass extinction in Earth's history!

The fifth was the extinction of the dinosaurs.

When a species disappears, that's the end. It will never reappear!

All is not lost! New, unknown creatures may be appearing in the ocean depths or in volcanic hot springs!

This sounds impossible. When life first appeared, the atmosphere contained no oxygen. It's indispensable for us, but it would immediately kill those new forms of life.

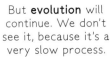

But **evolution** will continue. We don't see it, because it's a very slow process.

Will there be flying tigers?

Or dolphins as intelligent as we are?

We can imagine anything, but we can't foresee the future.

And us—will we evolve too?

Probably, but it will take tens or hundreds of thousands of years!

And the results will surely be different from what we imagine today!

I often dream about the inhabitants of the moon!

No one can live on the moon, because there is no atmosphere!

Life as we know it needs water. There is no longer any water on Mars, although life may have appeared there in the past, when rivers flowed on the planet.

On Mars, then. I also dream of Martians!

Elsewhere in the universe, anything is possible. Our galaxy contains more than 200 billion stars. Each of them is a sun orbited by several planets.

If a planet is at just the right distance from its sun, neither too hot nor too cold, there could be liquid water there, like there is on Earth.

What if life elsewhere were completely different? Electromagnetic or gaseous?

Why not? But life requires reproduction and transformation. Living creatures have to evolve, otherwise they're like streams or volcanoes, which move but aren't alive.

So there might be extraterrestrials up there!

Yes, but there's no reason they would resemble us. Given the diversity of life on Earth, it's likely they would be completely different from anything we can imagine!

GEOLOGIC TIME SCALE

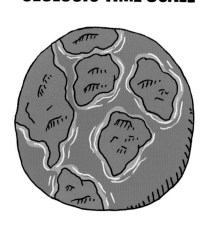

Period

0		
12,000 years ago		
2.6 million years ago		
5.3 million		
23 million		
34 million		
56 million		
66 million		
145 million		

Holocene

Pleistocene

Pliocene

Miocene

Oligocene

Eocene

Paleocene

Cretaceous

Jurassic

ERA

Quaternary

Tertiary

Secondary

CENOZOIC

MESOZOIC

Era/Eon	Period	Age
	Triassic	
PALEOZOIC (Primary)	Permian	252 million
	Carboniferous	299 million
	Devonian	359 million
	Silurian	419 million
	Ordovician	444 million
	Cambrian	485 million
PRECAMBRIAN	Proterozoic Eon	541 million
	Archean Eon	2.5 billion
	Hadean Eon	4 billion
		4.6 billion

GLOSSARY

Adaptation
Transformation of a species in the course of evolution, linked to a change in its environment. Adaptation results in better survival or more efficient re-production.

Amniotes
Vertebrates whose embryos develop within a membrane (the amniotic sac) inside an egg or the mother's womb. Includes all reptiles, birds, and mammals.

Amphibious
Said of an animal capable of living on land or in the water: frogs, hippopotamuses, etc.

Arborescent
Resembling a tree.

Arthropods
Animals that have an external skeleton and articulated legs: insects, spiders, crustaceans, millipedes . . .

Articulated
Made up of rigid parts that are connected and can move relative to each other.

Bacteria
Microorganisms consisting of single cells that are different from animal and plant cells, usually measuring only a few microns (thousandths of a millimeter).

Biodiveristy
The diversity of living creatures, often measured by the number of species present in the environment being studied.

Biped
Animal that normally moves about upright on its two rear legs.

Carbon
Chemical element found in the air and in certain rocks. It is an essential component of living creatures, whether microbes, plants, or animals.

Carnivore
Animal that feeds on the flesh of other animals.

Cell
Basic unit of all living creatures, which may consist of a single cell or a collection of cells. Single-celled animals are microscopic.

Chlorophyll
Green pigment present in most plants. It uses the sun's energy to make carbohydrates from carbon dioxide and water.

Coevolution
Parallel evolution of two species or two groups of living creatures that are connected with each other, for example flowers and the insects that pollinate them, or animals and their parasites.

Colony
Group of animals or microorganisms of the same species living in the same place. In certain cases, such as with bacteria or corals, the individuals of a colony are produced by budding and are all identical.

Colonization
Progressive occupation of a natural environment by a species or group of species.

Competition
Rivalry between two living creatures that seek the same resource, such as food or shelter.

Courtship Display
Movements or songs performed by an animal to attract a mate.

Diverge
Become different from each other, as in the case of two species descended from the same ancestral species.

Embryo
Animal at the beginning of its development in the egg or in its mother's womb, before the formation of its principal organs.

Evolution
Transformations of an animal or plant species over time. In a larger sense, evolution is also the history of life since its appearance on Earth.

Extinction
Disappearance of a species or group of species. A species is extinct when all individual members of the species are dead.

Fauna
All of the animals living at one time or in the same region.

Fossil
Remains of a plant or animal that are preserved after its death and slowly mineralized, turning into stone.

Gills
Respiratory organs of many aquatic animals, for example fish and crustaceans.

Glaciation
Period of Earth's history characterized by a cooling of the global climate and by the growth of ice caps.

Herbivore
Animal that feeds on plants (grasses, leaves, or roots).

Larva (plural Larvae)
Young animal very different in appearance from the adult. In the course of its development it undergoes one or more metamorphoses (transformations).

Magma
Molten rock at very high temperatures located deep below Earth's crust.

Meteorite
Rocky or metallic mass from outer space that falls onto Earth.

Microorganism
Very small living creature, visible with a microscope.

Molecule
A particle of a chemical substance; for example, a molecule of carbon dioxide or a molecule of sugar.

Organism
A living creature, or the body of a living creature.

Pangaea
The single continent at the beginning of the Jurassic, before its breakup into separate parts.

Photosynthesis
Production of carbohydrates by plants that possess chlorophyll, in the presence of sunlight.

Plankton
Creatures that live in suspension in seawater or freshwater.

Pollen
Male reproductive elements of a plant, equivalent to the spermatozoa of an animal.

Population
All the individuals of a species that live in the same region.

Predator
Animal that hunts other animals for food.

Prey
Animal that a predator catches for food.

Quadruped
Animal that normally moves about on four legs.

Scavenger
Animal that feeds on the dead bodies of animals that it did not itself kill.

Species
A group of living creatures capable of reproducing among themselves or descended from each other, for example **Tyrannosaurus rex** or **Homo sapiens**.

Vibrissa (plural Vibrissae)
Large, sensitive hair, for example a cat's "whisker."

Wingspan
Distance between the tips of the spread wings of a flying animal.

INDEX

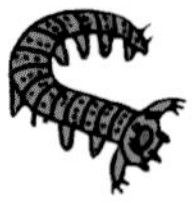

First published in Belgium by Casterman as L'Historie de la vie en BD T1. L'evolution de la naissance de la terre a nos jours – by Jean-Baptist de Panafieu & Adrienne Barman
Copyright © Casterman /2017
All Rights Reserved

English translation by George Newman
English translation copyright © 2020 by Holiday House Publishing, Inc.
All Rights Reserved
HOLIDAY HOUSE is registered in the U.S. Patent and Trademark Office.
Printed and bound in August 2020 at Toppan Leefung, DongGuan City, China.
www.holidayhouse.com
First Edition
1 3 5 7 9 10 8 6 4 2

Library of Congress Cataloging-in-Publication Data

Names: Panafieu, Jean-Baptiste de, author. | Barman, Adrienne, illustrator.

Title: History of the world in comics / written by Jean-Baptiste de Panafieu ; illustrated by Adrienne Barman.
Other titles: Histoire de la vie en BD. English
Description: First edition in English. | New York : Holiday House, [2020]
Originally published in French as L'Histoire de la vie en BD by Casterman. | Audience: Ages 10 and up | Audience: Grades 4-6 | Summary: «A paleontologist and a storyteller take two children through the birth of our planet to the present day, covering major geological periods and the evolution of life on Earth»—Provided by publisher.
Identifiers: LCCN 2019055031 | ISBN 9780823445783 (hardcover) ISBN 9780823445837 (paperback)
Subjects: LCSH: Life—Origin—Juvenile literature. | Evolution (Biology)—Juvenile literature. | Life—Origin—Comic books, strips, etc. | Comic books, strips, etc.—Juvenile literature.
Classification: LCC QH325 .P36 2020 | DDC 576.8/3—dc23
LC record available at https://lccn.loc.gov/2019055031

ISBN: 978-0-8234-4578-3 (hardcover)
ISBN: 978-0-8234-4583-7 (paperback)